Lace in Fashion

Lace in Fashion

FROM THE SIXTEENTH TO THE TWENTIETH CENTURIES

Pat Earnshaw

B.T. Batsford Ltd · *London*

© Pat Earnshaw 1985

First published 1985

ISBN 0 7134 4642 0

Typeset by Keyspools Ltd, Golborne, Lancashire
and printed in Great Britain by
Anchor Brendon Ltd, Tiptree, Essex

for the publishers
B.T. Batsford Ltd
4 Fitzhardinge Street
London W1H 0AH

Contents

Lace: A slender openwork fabric of linen, cotton, silk, woollen or metal threads, usually ornamented with inwrought or applied patterns. Often called after the place where it is manufactured.

(*Oxford English Dictionary*, Lace: 6)

Fashion: Conventional usage in dress, mode of life, style of speech etc., especially as observed in the upper circles of society, for the time being.

(*O.E.D.*, Fashion: 9,10)

Foreword

Lace which began, pre-fashion, as an incidental decoration of functional objects, became in the second half of the sixteenth century adapted as a fashionable insignium of Court and high society, and so achieved no function whatsoever except to decorate, enhance and discriminate the upper echelons who wore it. Even its beauty through the ages became for the most part subservient to this purpose.

This book aims to explore not only lace in fashion itself, but also the social conditions which promoted its success and, as they changed, eventually led to its downfall; the territorial wars tending to close one area of lace production and to open up another; the coordinating effect of the numerous intermarriages among the royal houses of Europe on lace and fashion; and the growing influence of the voice of the people. All these factors exerted the most powerful sway over the techniques, designs and textures of laces, and on how, when and where they were worn.

P.E
Guildford 1984

Note: to avoid confusion, the author would like to make clear that her use of the title *Lace in Fashion* dates from 1983, when she presented a series of lectures under this title, in England and abroad.

Photographic Acknowledgements

Figs 78, 123a, 123b are reproduced by gracious permission of Her Majesty Queen Elizabeth II; and fig. 111 by permission of Her Royal Highness the Princess of Wales.

Joslyn Baker, figs 53c, 101. Berlei (UK) Ltd, figs 145, 146. Bibliothèque Nationale, Paris, fig. 49. Bomann-Museum, Celle, fig. 47b. British Museum, London, figs 17, 147. Budleigh Salterton Museum, fig. 151a. Caroline Charles, fig. 113. Chertsey Museum, figs 69b, 69e, 74, 82a, 86a. Christie's, London, figs 25b, 35b, 36, 39a, 39b, 43, 44a, 47a, 51, 59, 60b, 69a, 83b, 90, 114, 125, 127, 128a,b,c, 132. City Art Gallery, Manchester, fig. 155. Cocoa, Cheltenham, fig. 112a. Condé Nast Publications Ltd, fig. 109. Dansk Folkemuseum, Nationalmuseet, figs. 61b, 62, 148a. Deutsche Bundesbank, fig. 3. Dover Publications Inc., figs 2b, 12. Embroiderers' Guild, Adelaide, fig. 99. Photographie Giraudon, figs 14, 60a, 115, 152. Alfred Godet, fig. 148b. Guildhall Library, London, fig. 41. Lise Helvard, fig. 82b. Hillwood, Washington DC, fig. 63a. Rachel Kay-Shuttleworth collection, fig. 80. Killerton House, fig. 94. G. Kramer, Amsterdam, fig. 149a. Kunstmuseum Basel, Kupferstichkabinett, fig. 4. Kunsthistorisches Museum, Vienna, figs 44b, 98, 129. Kyoto Costume Institute, figs 84, 86b. Erich Lessing/Magnum Photos and the John Hillelson Agency, colour plate 2. Marisa Martin, fig. 108. Marian May, figs 138a, 141. Metropolitan Museum of Art, figs 33b, 70. Musées Nationaux, figs 5, 33a, 56. Museo del Prado, Madrid, fig. 15. Museum of Fine Arts, Boston, figs 9, 130. National Portrait Gallery, London, figs 11, 21, 29, 38a,b, 58a, 61a, 73, 133, 154a. Norton Simon Museum of Art, Pasadena, fig. 65. Osterreichisches Museum, Vienna, fig. 38c. The Earl of Oxford and Asquith, fig. 18. Phillips, London, figs 19, 68, 91, 118, 149b, colour plate 4. Pierpoint Morgan Library, fig. 156. Rijksmuseum, figs. 46, 52, 123c. Roger-Viollet, Paris, figs 31a, 31c, 34, 37, 42, 45, 48, 121a, 135. Royal Pavilion, Art Gallery and Museums, Brighton, fig. 75. Marquess of Salisbury, fig. 24. Sammlungen des Fürsten von Liechtenstein, Schloss Vaduz, fig. 1. Sotheby Parke Bernet and Co., London, figs 25a, 27, 30, 55, 102, 134, 151b, colour plate 1. © 1984 Sotheby Parke Bernet Inc., New York, figs 32, 150. Staatsgemäldesammlungen, Munich, figs 10, 22. Stadt- und Kantonsbibliothek Vadiana St Gallen, photo: Zentralbibliothek, Zurich, figs 7, 8. Tate Gallery, London, fig. 35a. Textile Conservation Centre, Hampton Court Palace, figs 54a, b. Towneley Hall Art Gallery and Museum, Burnley Borough Council, colour plate 3. Lillie Trivett, fig. 92. Alice Tucker, Melbourne, Australia, fig. 58b. Victoria and Albert Museum, London, figs 6, 13, 26, 28, 31b, 50, 66, 72, 126. Gemäldegalerie der Akademie der bildenden Künste in Wien, fig. 63b. Worcester Art Museum, Ma., fig. 40. All other photographs are by Ronald Brown.

Cover illustrations: (front) Sotheby Parke Bernet and Co., London; (back) National Detnational historiske Museum, på Frederiksborg, Denmark.

I

Before 1600

THE EMERGENCE OF FASHION

Fashion, like lace itself, is a word of many meanings. In its general sense of a particular shape, style or pattern, a way of doing things, a custom characteristic of a particular place or period of time, it can be traced back to *c*.1300. In the fifteenth century men and women of fashion were associated by their high quality or breeding, and recognized by their conformity in expenditure and habits. By the mid-sixteenth century they could be recognized also by their conformity in dress.

This visual aspect of the person of fashion strengthened through the following decades. In 1568, for example, we read of 'a scarlet Robe with a hoode (as the fashion then was)'. By 1600 the modern concept of fashion was in full flood: 'her luve is ... as unconstant as the fashion'; and by 1654, 'Fashions crosse the Seas as oft as the Packet Boat.'[1]

Clothes had become an immediately recognizable symbol of the wearer's exclusiveness, like a military uniform or a nun's habit, but on an immensely grander scale – and a fickle one. Thus to remain exclusive the wearer had to adhere quickly and unquestioningly to every arbitrary change, however frequent and however erratic.

The evolution of this concept of fashion coincided very closely with the evolution of lace as a fashion fabric which was to become at times so important that it almost dominated the entire scene.

Though lace seems to have erupted as inexplicably as the outward explosion of a bud into a flower, yet just as that bud would have developed through a long, near-dormant history, so all the main techniques, or methods, of lace-making were in existence, in embryo, many years before they blossomed so lavishly over the clothes of men and women.

Fashion laces in all their huge variety were, every one of them, slender, decorative and made of threads combined together to make an openwork structure. The laces which preceded them were by contrast stout, utilitarian and not particularly decorative, but still openwork and still made of threads. Coarse fishing nets, knotted at the corner of every square, had only to dwindle to a delicate texture, to be embroidered by hand with sophisticated or ingenuous designs, and they became a lace called filet, or lacis. The strong woven gauzes used in Italy for sieving flour and known as buratto had only to be copied in a fine silk to become a slender openwork fabric, in effect a lace, either patterned or plain.

The techniques of those archaic laces were of two basic kinds: using one thread, and using many threads. This simple distinction produced two quite different types of lace.

Single-thread laces originated in embroidery which, though defined as the surface decoration of a woven or other pre-existing fabric, can include openwork, and when there is enough openwork it may be called a lace. Drawnwork and cutwork are two examples of embroidered laces of great importance to lace in fashion in the sixteenth century. Openwork embroidery, carried to its extreme, led to a lace without any fabric foundation at all. Still made with a single thread, manipulated by a needle into loops like varied buttonhole stitches, it became a needle lace.

Many-thread laces used a variable number of threads, from eight to over 1000, all of limited length. They were fixed at the top of the work and then knotted, plaited, twisted or crossed, and so converted into laces such as macramé or bobbin lace. The name bobbin lace derived from its use of small thread-holders made of bone, wood and occasionally metal, which acted as weights to keep the threads at an even tension, and as handles so that the thread itself did not need to be touched. Bobbins were also used from ancient times for making macramé and for closed braiding, as they are today – two techniques which sometimes made use of a supporting pillow just as bobbin laces always did.

The evidence that all these techniques – for embroidery, needle laces, macramé, and for braiding if not for actual bobbin laces – go back at least 2,000 years, is sparse but unquestionable. Macramé

1 *A simple seaming lace, made with bobbins, and joining together the shoulder and sleeves of the monk's habit. 'The Adoration of the King', Hugo van der Goes, c.1482.*

fringing is carved on Assyrian tunics in the sandstone rocks above the ancient ruins of Ninevah;[2] drawnwork is found on the burial clothes of Egyptian mummies from around 1000 BC; hair nets and knotted bags lie in wait for the resurrection of their embalmed bodies; and caps of buttonhole stitches, like needle lace destitute of design, warm the skulls of skeletons in the 3,000-year-old bog graves near Copenhagen in Denmark.[3]

It was not, however, until a few hundred years ago that laces became slender, and it is this fineness of texture rather than any significant variation of technique which marks them as fashion laces. During the long quiescent period the main use of lace was for church furnishing, or seaming together the woven widths of household linens (fig. 1).

Fig. 2a shows with amazing precision a similar seaming lace, this time joining the front and back of a cushion of c.1340. The cushion cover itself is

pierced with cutwork decoration, too widely spaced to constitute a lace fabric, yet indistinguishable in kind from the cutwork which was to cover the entire surface of the elaborate ruffs worn more than 200 years later (figs 2b, 21).

Lace is not mentioned in the English sumptuary edict of 1482[4] which aimed to restrict silks, velvets, precious metals, damasks and satins to the upper classes. For example: 'That no man under the estate of a Duke wear any cloth of gold or tissue upon pain of forfeiting for every offence, 20 marks' (1 mark = $\frac{2}{3}$ £).

In 1483 an inventory of the goods of Bartolo di Tura of Siena[5] refers to a lady's silk coif worked in *reticelle* (little networks). Such coifs, or hair nets, were elaborate at that time, often made of gold thread knotted into small diamond shapes (fig. 3). They appear in many portraits and engravings of the early sixteenth century and, while not strictly a fashion, since they seem not to have been the prerogative of an upper circle of society, they were a kind of lace.

Ten years later, another inventory was drawn up in Milan, that of the sisters Angela and Ippolita Sforza-Visconti:

Velleto uno d'oro filato.
Payro uno fodrete di cambria lavorate a gugia.
Lenzuolo uno di revo di tele cinque lavorato a punto.
Peza una de tarnete d'argento facte a stelle.
Lenzuolo uno de tele, quatro lavorato a radexelo.
Peze quatro de radexelo per mettere ad uno moscheto.
Tarneta una d'oro et seda negra facta da ossi.
Pecto uno d'oro facto a grupi.
Lavoro uno de rechamo facto a grupi, dove era suso le perle de Madona Biancha.
Binda una lavarata a poncto de doii fuxi per uno lenzuolo.

Milan, 12 September, 1493. (Quoted from Hudson Moore.)

The inventory's precise significance is open to speculation, and must remain so, since all translations to some extent allow alternative meanings for words, but a number of items suggest a reference to lace; for example the *radexelo* on a sheet (*lenzuolo*) may mean cutwork as in the cushion cover against which Pax is leaning in the Siena fresco. In the next line, however, the *radexelo* is put on a mosquito net (*moscheto*). The *tarneta d'oro seda negra facta da ossi* (gold and black silk braid made with bones), and the flounce worked with 12 bobbins (*doii fuxi*), suggest what they say – a fabric made with bobbins, but there is no evidence that the fabric was openwork, or that it was bobbin lace rather than macramé; indeed the breast cloth of knotted gold (*pecto uno d'oro facto a grupi*) sounds more like macramé, or even filet.

2 (a) A mural from the Palazzo Pubblico in Siena showing the allegorical figure of Pax (Peace) reclining against a cushion embroidered with cutwork. Lorenzetti, Siena, c.1340.

(b) A cutwork design to be repeated in each segment of a ruff, from the pattern book of Vinciolo, 1587.

3 A netted coif worn by Elsbeth Tucher of Nuremberg, by Albrecht Dürer, 1499. For the rich the coif would be of gold or silk studded with pearls and jewels, for the poor of horsehair.

It was in the second half of the sixteenth century that lace in fashion began to awaken, and it is interesting to trace the escalation of portents which heralded its coming. Engravings, woodcuts and paintings all illustrate this evolution, which is demonstrated with exquisite precision in the miniatures of the Tudor Court, as sharp and clear as an idealized reality.

A drawing of 1520 by Holbein (fig. 4) portrays the chemise or smock emerging above a lady's bodice into a high embroidered neckline, which then turns outwards in a little frill, a tiny progenitor which would grow into the huge circular ruffs of 40 years later.

In 1539 Holbein the Younger went to Germany to paint a portrait of Anne of Cleves, intended to help Henry VIII decide whether he would like her for his fourth bride (fig. 5). The forehead-piece, beneath an elaborate pearl-encrusted coif of a type known as the French hood, shows a drawnwork design which closely resembles the Liberta pattern of Vavassore's book, published in Venice c.1530. The message 'A bon fine' sounds like a *memento mori*, 'May she come to a good end' or 'Happy ending', an apposite sentiment bearing in mind the King's deadly record, and perhaps an effective one, since Anne managed later to be parted from him by divorce instead of decapitation.

Henry's first wife, Catherine of Aragon, is some-

4 *Middle-class female costume in Basle, c.1520, by Holbein. The linen shift is extensively exposed over the back and shoulders, with a high frilled neckline.*

times credited with the introduction of bobbin lace into England, but there is no real evidence of its manufacture in England before about 1580, though the existence of bobbin laces in Venice and in Switzerland in 1536 – the year in which Catherine died – seems clear enough. On the other hand, her Spanish upbringing would have made her proficient at embroidery, and her sister Joanna the Mad left at her death large numbers of drawnwork and filet samplers, which are types of embroidered lace.

Some ambiguity must also surround the 'ell of German latticework' (approximately 54 inches) ordered in 1543 by Eleanor of Austria, daughter of Joanna the Mad, and sister of the Holy Roman Emperor Charles V, who married François I of France in 1530 as his second wife.[6] The appearance of this lace may possibly be that shown in fig. 6, where one would suspect a bobbin lace, though the word 'latticework' in itself could equally describe a knotted filet.

Little help is given by the 'German networks' associated with Barbara Uttman of Annaberg, in the Erzegebirge Mountains, who lived from 1514 to 1575. Though her husband was a master miner, and the miners wore hair nets made by the local women, this in no way proves that latticework meant network. Such bobbin and needle laces as existed in 1543 were unambiguously geometric, with the impression of strands running together and separating in a formally intersecting manner.

A painting, dated 1545, of the Protestant reformer Joachim von Watt, known as Vadianus of St Gall, shows the full top of his shirt gathered into a band of lace indicated by the simplest of trellis-like cross-hatching, which could very appropriately be called latticework (fig. 7). It corresponds closely with some designs in a book of bobbin lace patterns, collated by a lady known only by her initials, R.M., and printed by Froschauer in Zurich in 1561 (fig. 8). The preface describes bobbin lace-making as having been introduced into Switzerland from Venice in 1536. While it decries indulgence in needless vanities, it specifies that many of the designs are to be constructed in gold and silver threads, or in coloured silks, for the excesses of the few must not spoil the enjoyment of the many, 'just as the vinegrower will not neglect his vineyard although persons misuse the vine daily and drink over the need' (translated by Claire Burkhard).

This Zurich pattern book also provides a prototype for the bobbin lace shown in fig. 9 which, in addition, can be matched with patterns in the Venetian *Le Pompe* of 1557. The post-dating poses no problem since these books, like many of their contemporaries, were not so much presentations of original designs as collections of traditional ones already in existence in the form of peasant laces, which were now being upgraded for middle-class wear by the use of richer materials.

In the painting of Claude, Duchess of Lorraine (fig. 10), needle laces begin to appear, bridging the gap between incidental clothes-decoration and the headier world of fashion; and it was needle laces which first established themselves for Court wear, rather than bobbin laces which for a while longer remained simple and 'lower class'. In this vivid portrait, every detail of the heavy, intensely human, face appears, depicted with a brilliant eye for living detail. The ruff is small but sharply delineated, and bears no more than a narrow fish-scale border of purling. Even the starry cutwork revealed by the open neck of the bodice is modest and sober, yet the wilful extravagance of the times was becoming poised to take off into the huge, awkward, excruciating millstones worn by Queen Elizabeth I and her courtiers, only a few years later (fig. 11).

Simple as the cutworks worn by Claude might appear, they were nonetheless constructed with the

5 *Anne of Cleves by Holbein, 1539. The forehead piece is embroidered with drawnwork and bears the message* A bon fine.

minutest of care, and so were time-consuming and very expensive. As early as 1555, Mary Tudor passed a law not only limiting the wearing of cutworks, but also restricting their importation.[7] Ruffles of cutwork 'made or wrought *out of* England' were forbidden to anyone under the degree of baron, while 'passement lace of gold or silver' and 'white-workes alias cut-workes, made beyond the sea' were forbidden to ladies lower than the wives of knights. Passements were straight-edged braids, similar to insertion or seaming laces, but made to be stitched flat around or across a garment, replacing embroideries which had the disadvantage of being embedded in the cloth, and so immovable. As fashion began to emerge, openwork passements were given a dentate or scalloped edge, and were called 'passemens dentellés' (literally, toothed laces). They could now be used as edgings, to ruffs and cuffs in particular, and their name was soon abbreviated to *dentelles*, a term which was adopted in 1598 as the name in French for all kinds of bobbin and needle laces.

The precise cost of the cutworks mentioned in the 1555 edict is hard to calculate. Wardrobe

6 *Eleanor of Austria (1498–1558) by Thomas de Leu, c.1543. The tight bodice line of the dress is emphasized by a band of simple black lace, probably made with bobbins since black was almost never used for needle laces.*

accounts of Mary I's sister Elizabeth in 1586 record cutwork for a ruff 'edged with good white lace' at 10s a yard, or nearly £20 in present day values (see page 155).[8] However, in 1560 Elizabeth had reformed the currency, making a profit of £50,000 in the process. For at least 15 years before that the country's economy had been in a mess, following Henry VIII's repeated debasements of the silver coinage – from 11 oz to 9 oz, then 6 oz, and finally 4 oz, between 1542 and 1547 (Porteus).[9]

As for the source of these cutworks, they are likely to have been made throughout Europe though perhaps, commercially, more especially in Flanders, Italy and France. England must also have had some ability in this field, for otherwise the import restrictions would have stood no chance at all of success.

The decorations of the sixteenth-century shirts and chemises progressed from high but very narrow frilled collars to gadrooned partlets sprouting like stiff bracket fungi from the circumference of the neck. They were at first quite plain, or had just a simple border of purling; but cutwork decoration, beginning at the outer border, spread eventually to cover the entire ruff, while at the same time the purling enlarged into a punto in aria fence of almost infinite variety. Frederic de Vinciolo's pattern book, published in Paris in 1587 and dedicated to Louise of Lorraine, wife of Catherine de' Medici's third son Henri III, is an invaluable record of this

7 *Vadianus of St Gall, aged 59, in 1545. The low circular neck of his shirt is tightly gathered into a band of latticework lace.*

8 *Woodcuts from the Zurich pattern book, by R.M., which match approximately the bobbin laces shown in figs 6, 7 and 9. Though not printed until 1561, some of the book's designs probably date from at least two decades earlier.*

9 *Detail from a portrait of a lady attributed to Lucus Cranach the younger, of Saxony, 1549. The wide cuffs of her undergarment are bordered with lace; compare fig. 8, row one.*

early fashion lace, and also for tracing the development from the embroidered lace, cutwork/reticella, into the needle lace stitches in the air (*punto in aria*) worked over and between outlining threads without a supporting cloth to contain them (fig. 12).

By the third quarter of the sixteenth century the partlets had expanded into circular ruffs so huge and cumbersome that they were known as millstones. No longer could they be part of other garments, for their mode of washing was an art in itself. They were now separate objects, tied around the neck, and quite staggeringly elaborate:

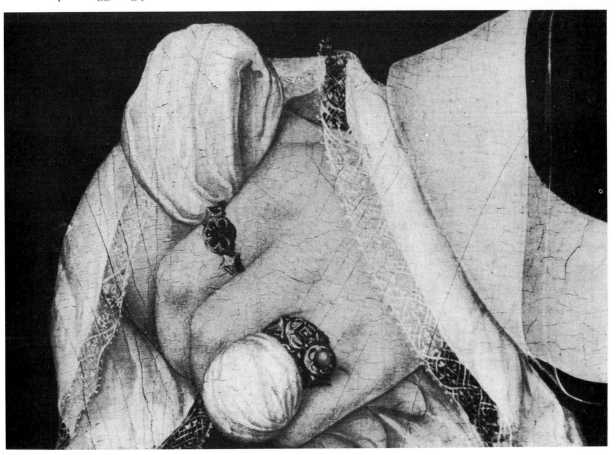

CLAVDIA HENRICI II REGIS GALLÆ   FILIA CAROLI III
LOTHARINGIÆ DVCIS   CONIVIX

10 *Claude, daughter of Henri II of France, and wife of Charles III, Duke of Lorraine, by Clouet, c.1562. Her shift appears to be of silk gauze continued upwards into a simply fluted ruff which turns outwards over a jewelled necklace. The exposed lining of her overgown reveals an exquisite border of cutwork edged with purling.*

clogged with gold, silver, or silk lace of stately price, wrought all over with needleworke; speckeled and sparkeled here and there with the sun, moone and starres, and many other antiques rare to behold. Some were wrought with openwork [cutwork] down to the middle of the ruff and further, some with close-worke [surface embroidery], some with purled lace. . . .[10]

Supported by underproppers and starch, the millstones fairly bristled with lace. In fact they quite literally bristled. The little teeth around the outside, outgrowths of the original purling, were sharp and could slash the cheek with an incautious turn – as if intended to keep others at a distance, as indeed socially they were. 'Not so close, thy breath will draw my ruff',[11] warns a gallant of the period, for the moist warmth of expired air at close quarters would soften its stiffening.

The need to keep the ruffs in perfect form and extension was so inexorable that Henri III pressed and prepared not only his ruffs but those of his most intimate friends with his own hands. The pro-

11 *Queen Elizabeth I, by J. Bettes the younger, c.1585–90. Her complex millstone ruff is supported by wires which radiate from her neck as underproppers. A single layer of cutwork edges the ruff which is closely toothed with punto in aria tinted with gold.*

digious amount of work involved can be appreciated by looking at a portrait such as fig. 22, and imagining each flute being washed, starched, curved and pressed, each fang of lace crisped and sharpened, the whole wheel set into perfect symmetry to spring outwards from a stiff supporting band around the neck.

While millstone ruffs were undoubtedly the most prestigious for formal wear, they did not monopolize the fashion scene. In 1577 Henri III was wearing a 'shirt collar turned down in the Italian style', similar to that worn by the romantic lover in fig. 13, dated 1588. At much the same time, however, Henri is also described as giving a series of entertainments at Court in which he appeared 'dressed as a woman with his bodice open displaying his chest, wearing a pearl necklace and three ruffs as did the women at Court' (Pierre de l'Estoile, *Journal*).[12] These 'three ruffs' would no doubt be similar in form to the early seventeenth-century triple ruff shown in fig. 22. A really complex one could consume up to 24 yards of lace which, at the price of cutwork quoted on page 14, would cost the equivalent of some £480 today.

Quite a variety of collars appears in an engraving of Henri IV, who married Henri III's sister Marguerite de Valois in 1572. Henri himself wears a small millstone edged with purling, and his young son a lace-edged shirt collar turned down over his doublet. The mother wears an open ruff of several tiers decorated with a single row of cutwork, while the nurse has a standing collar bordered with punto in aria (fig. 14).

This engraving is of additional interest in that it exists in two forms, which are mirror images of each other. The one illustrated here extols the virtues of Marie de' Medici whom Henri married in 1600 after his divorce from Marguerite. The other appears to refer to Henri's family life with his mistress Gabrielle d'Estrées, whom he had intended to marry, had she not died unexpectedly in 1599. She bore Henri three children: César in 1594, Catherine Henriette in 1596, and Alexandre in 1598. The verse with fig. 14 reads, in extract: 'France, you see in this little tableau, All your happiness and good fortune. It is your Henri. . . . You see also the Queen . . . Medici, his lawful wife . . . their little gift from God, the Dauphin. . . .' The mirror-image engraving also has a verse: '. . . the children of the Monarch, By God's will the son resembles the father* . . . he is the Hercules and Mars of the French . . . one does not yet see Alexandre estre . . .',[13] that is Alexander-to-be, as if the engraving had been made before his birth. Though *estre* is the old form of *être* (to be), it

* The term 'filz de père' (son of the father) was used to indicate illegitimacy.

could also be construed as a play on *Estrées*.

From the point of view of lace fashion it would obviously be helpful to know the precise date of the engravings. 1602 has been postulated, but it is inappropriate for either. The date must lie between just prior to 1598, when Alexandre was born, and 1605, when Marie's first child, Louis (XIII) would have been four years old.

Apart from this social enigma, the inventory taken at the death of Gabrielle d'Estrées (1599) provides illumination of the cost of lace in fashion at the end of the sixteenth century:

Item, five handkerchiefs worked with gold, silver, and silk, valued at one hundred crowns.

Item, two towels, also worked with gold and silver, and appraised at one hundred crowns.

Item, three towels of white drawn-work, valued altogether at thirty crowns.

Item, one pair of cuffs of cut-work enriched with silver, valued at twenty crowns.

Item, two white handkerchiefs of cut-work, valued together at twenty crowns.

All these towels and handkerchiefs, which were found in the little coffer which the said defunct lady usually carried with her to Court, are remaining in the hands of Sieur de Beringhen, according to the command of His Majesty, to whom she had promised these things should be returned.

(Quoted from Hudson Moore.)

13 *Probably Lord Thomas Howard, by Nicholas Hilliard, 1588. The shirt collar, turned down over the doublet, shows a pattern of 'ouvrage de point coupe' which might also have come from Vinciolo's book. The clasped hands symbolize plighted troth and platonic love, as does the motto 'Of friendship therefore of love'.*

12 *A pattern for cutwork ('ouvrage de point coupe') published in Paris by Vinciolo in 1587, and intended for use on a ruff, or a shift. The bird pecking a cherry, and the extended snail, are typical designs of the late Elizabethan and Jacobean periods.*

The French monetary unit, the crown (*écu d'or*) may in general be estimated at approximately five shillings (25p), though it was a gold coin as opposed to the gold and silver of the English crown (see page 155). Thus for the first item, 100 crowns would be equivalent to £25 or, if this is updated to current values by a factor of 40, an impressive £1,000. The fourth item, a pair of cutwork cuffs, becomes £200; and the fifth, two white handkerchiefs of cutwork, also £200, or £100 each. Thus translated, it no longer seems inconceivably undignified that the King of France should ask to have back from the estate of his dead mistress his gift of seven handkerchiefs, five towels, and pair of cuffs.

Handkerchiefs were indeed prestigious objects, and no mere rags for wiping the nose. They are shown in many portraits of the second half of the sixteenth century, prominently displayed as in the Cranach portrait of 1549 (fig. 9), and in the painting of Isabella in 1579 (fig. 15). Isabella was the daughter of Philip II of Spain by his third wife, Elizabeth de Valois. She married in 1599 the Archduke Albert of Austria, a union intended to secure the Netherlands as a Spanish dominion. This comprised the areas of Flanders (approximately equivalent to Belgium) and the Northern Provinces, including Holland. Though the Provinces had declared their freedom in 1581, it was not formally acknowledged by Spain until the Treaty of Munster in 1648.

A magnificent wedding present for the Habsburg couple was a large coverlet of bobbin lace, reputedly given by the lace-makers of Brabant. It shows a mixture of closely textured wholestitch, and plaited strands, the parts linked by sewings, and is of an amazing proficiency of technique considering that the first bobbin lace pattern book to be printed in Flanders had appeared only two years before, in Liège. The book contained no original material, which might indicate that there were no truly local designs. One of the busy trade routes from Venice passed via Switzerland to Flanders, and in that way both the Venetian *Le Pompe* and the Zurich R.M. may have passed northwards.

The squared appearance of the wedding coverlet is reminiscent of a cutwork technique, which had developed in the later sixteenth century into a mixed lace sometimes known as reticella. This was made entirely independently of any woven fabric, by using plaited strands to make frames within which needle lace decorations were then suspended. It was only a short step onwards to make the entire thing, frames and fillings, by plaiting, as in some Genoese laces which strikingly resemble reticella insertion, or punto in aria edging (fig. 16).

The practical apron, like the utilitarian handkerchief, had also an up-market form, which resembled that worn by the little girl in fig. 14. None of the portraits of adults here show aprons and it was perhaps at this time not quite an upper circle of society fashion, as it later became. Stephen Gossons in 1596 aims his *Pleasant Quippes* at the vanity, not of the Court itself, but of the 'Upstart Newfangled Gentlewomen': 'These aprons white of finest thread, So choicely tied, so dearly bought, So finely fringed, so nicely spread, So quaintlie cut, so richly wrought....'[14] 'Tied' refers to the strings with their decorative tassels embellished with gold and silver thread; 'dearly bought' to their high cost; 'finely fringed' to the punto in aria border; 'quaintlie cut' to the cutwork decoration; and 'richly wrought' to the needle lace stitches filling the cut-out portions, with perhaps some surface embroidery.

Few original aprons are likely to have survived from this period, but the design for one was copied in the early twentieth century by the Aemilia Ars

14 *Henri IV* en famille, *by Gautier after Le Clerc, c.1598. The boy on the left wears a turn-down shirt collar, as in fig. 13, and the traditional sword hangs from his belt. The mother wears a front-opening ruff, and the nurse a standing collar. The infant, barely two years old, has her chest encased in rigid stays and her skirt supported by a farthingale.*

Society of Bologna from a pattern in Passarotti's book of 1591. In a photograph, the apron looks sufficiently compact to be original, but in fact it is quite gross, the thicker thread which was used swelling the border to a gargantuan size. Apart from this anomaly its late origin is confirmed by the tassels being worked over electric wire, to give them form and stiffness, where the original would have used gold.

Lace was also worn on coifs, and one is shown in an engraving of Mary Queen of Scots (fig. 17). Mary's passion for the monotones of black and white no doubt owed much to Spanish influence, not only because it was strong in fashion at that time, but also because of Mary's wish, after the death in 1561 of her French husband François II, to marry Don Carlos, son of Philip II of Spain by his first marriage. Don Carlos had early been affianced to Elizabeth de Valois but on the death of Mary Tudor in 1558, Philip himself took Elizabeth as his third wife. Don Carlos, however, was quite violently insane at times, and the Scottish Queen's intentions came to nothing.

Many portraits shown Mary wearing a veil, which was also a style of this period. Such a veil would be of woven gauze, a plain or patterned buratto – see *velleto uno d'oro filato* (a veil of gold thread) in the Sforza inventory of 1493 (page 10). One, reputedly hers, is of translucent silk chequered with heavier strands, and caught to an inner lining by a tiny golden sequin at the corner of each square (fig. 18). It measures approximately three feet by six feet, and it was perhaps just such a veil that the unhappy Queen wore at her execution in 1587 when, aged 44, with almost half her life gone in imprisonment, she went to her beheading. She is describing as being dressed in black satin save for a long white lace-edged veil which flowed down her back to the ground, and a starched white coif bordered with bone lace. Before she knelt at the block, her black overgarment was removed, revealing a scarlet petticoat and bodice. Two red sleeves – which were often separately attached – were then put on.[15]

A similar veil may have been among the New Year gifts to Queen Elizabeth in 1578: 'A veil with spangles and small bone lace of silver'. The gifts also

15 *The infanta Isabella, by Sanchez Coello, 1579. In this early portrait, her use of lace is restrained and delicate, her clothes exceedingly modest. The high collar of her Spanish gown pushes the little ruff up to just beneath her chin. Its sharp spikes of punto in aria, and inner line of cutwork, are precisely matched by the small pendant cuffs, and the trimming of the handkerchief which she holds.*

16 *The differing techniques of needle, bobbin and mixed laces making 'little networks' (reticella): (top) Cutwork, the squares cut from a woven fabric, then filled with buttonhole stitches; (centre) Reticella, the outlines of the squares made of plaited thread, or needle-woven strands, the decoration by buttonhole stitches; (bottom) Bobbin lace, probably Genoese, built up of plaited strands arranged in squares, with leaves (point d'esprit ovales) and compact wholestitch imitating a border of woven linen pierced with cutwork.*

included 'A swete bag with small bone lace of gold' (fig. 19).

Thus the sixteenth century ended with lace already established around necks and wrists, on handkerchiefs, veils and aprons, and around women's heads. The fashions were stiff, ungainly and torturingly uncomfortable. The general compulsive lavishness, verging on decadence, which had overtaken clothes is strikingly conveyed by John Donne in his *Paradoxes and Problems*, published in 1633, though almost certainly written around 1600:

A fool if he come into a Princes Court and see a gay man leaning at a wall, so glistering, and so painted in many colours that he is hardly discernable from one of the pictures in the Arras [tapestry] hanging, his body like

an Iron-bound chest, girt in, and thick ribb'd with broad gold laces, may (and commonly doth) envy him.[16]

'Painted' refers to the practice of plastering the skin with white, often using a mercury or lead compound, then touching the cheeks and lips with red; the 'Iron-bound chest' refers to the iron corset which produced in men and women a tubular torso topping in one case the forked trunk hose, and in the other the bell-shaped farthingale. The lavishness of the 'broad gold laces' went with the general puffed and scaffolded line of the clothes which formed, as it were, a display board on which silks, velvets, jewels, embroideries and lace could be hung for exhibition.

The gold and silver laces so copiously worn were of necessity simple in construction because of the stiff intractability of the threads, in which narrow bands of foil were wound spirally around a core of yellow silk using a purling wheel. They were worked with bobbins to prevent the sweat of the hands from tarnishing the metal. Some of this

17 *Mary Queen of Scots with her cousin and second husband, Lord Darnley, c.1565. She wears a lace-trimmed coif dipping forward over the centre of her forehead. Her head is framed by a huge veil or conch which billows around her and then falls to the ground. Though the size of the squares and the magnitude of the lace border are grossly exaggerated in the engraving, they have their counterpart in fig. 18.*

18 *Detail from a veil reputedly belonging to Mary. The openwork leno (buratto) weave is clearly seen, also the tiny sequins similar to those which appear in a contemporary painting of Marguerite de Valois, by Clouet. A seaming lace joins the veil to a later added border around which a tiny dentate bobbin lace imitates the original.*

19 *Detail from a painting of the Amsterdam school,*
1610–20. The large cuffs are edged with bobbin lace, and
the lady carries a 'swete bag with small bone lace of gold'.

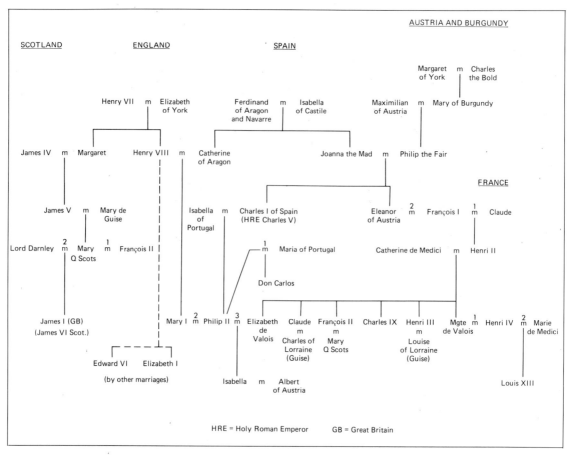

20 *The interrelations of royal and noble houses in the sixteenth century, which facilitated a uniformity of fashion throughout the Courts of Europe.*

passementerie was so rich, and so valuable, that it was moved from one dress or doublet to another, and inventoried under jewellery. Henri III of France wore 4,000 yards of gold lace, on what must have been an extraordinarily heavy suit, to impress the Diet of Blois in 1577.[17] This meeting of the States General was an attempt to remedy the high rate of inflation which had shaken France's economy in the years between 1549 and 1576. The increased cost of living was blamed on shipments of bullion from America – and Henri must have looked as though quite some quantity of this incumbency had attached itself to his person.

An astounding extravagance had been in the air even back in 1535, expressed in the fantasies of François Rabelais in *Gargantua*, with his descriptions of 'caps or bonnets of black velvet adorned with jewels and buttons of gold, and a white plume parted by so many rows of gold spangles, at the end whereof hung dangling in a more sparkling resplendency rubies, emeralds and diamonds.'[18]

Blum quotes from a discourse on the reasons for

the high cost of living in France in 1586: 'Gentlemen all go dressed in gold, silver, velvet, satin or taffeta; their mills, their lands, their meadows, their woods, and their revenues are all swallowed up and consumed in habiliments. . . .'[19] In 1599 Ben Jonson commented that men 'thought little of turning 400 or 500 acres of their best land into two or three trunks of apparel'.[20] Elizabeth I at her death in 1603 left 3,000 jewel-encrusted gowns.[21]

Lace was already but one huge extravagance among a plethora of others. Did it matter to those sixteenth-century wearers that linen laces were also delicate and beautiful works of art which were expensive, not for their thread as were the much simpler and more quickly constructed gold and silver laces, but because of the lifespans of women which their manufacture consumed? It seems unlikely.

During the following century lace was to spread rapidly to shoes and knees for men, and to bosoms and skirts for women.

2

The Seventeenth Century

THE DIVINE RIGHT OF KINGS

1600–1625

The needle laces, punto in aria and cutwork or reticella, established on costume by the end of the sixteenth century, made a smooth and almost imperceptible transition into the seventeenth. In 1603 when Elizabeth I died, James VI of Scotland succeeded her as James I of Great Britain. His native Court had been an impoverished one, and it might be supposed that this sudden expectation of wealth – Elizabeth's allowance had been £300,000 a year during the last ten years of her reign[1] – went a little to the heads of the new King and his consort Anne of Denmark. In 1609 there are references to 'treble-quadruple Daedalian ruffes' and 'stiff-necked Rebatoes, that have more arches for pride than five London Bridges'. The extravagant similes eloquently convey the deified atmosphere of the Court where great ruffs, supported by rigid under-proppers, were raised tier upon tier in huge arches giving the appearance of that archaic labyrinth within which Daedalus of Crete housed the deadly Minotaur. The association of legend and monarchy was a natural one: a heady conviction of the divine right of kings evoked an ambience of untouchable glory in which they could do no wrong.

In 1604 a patent for the making of 'Venice gold and silver thread', to run for 21 years, was granted by James I to Richard Dike. Such thread was used for braids, passements, and the loops of purling which gave a shining rim to the ruff's curved flutings. By 1622 it was being derided by the Dutch as a 'great waste of bullion'. The fact was that the product was so much more valuable than the gold coins which bought it that these were being clipped, or entirely melted down, to provide the metal foil to twist around silk to make the thread, to the great detriment of the country's finances. By 1624 James was forced to prohibit the use of gold purls 'as tending to the consumption of the coin and bullion of the kingdom'.[2]

In France, during the first decade, Henri IV imposed a restraining influence. He liked to wear plain – or relatively plain – clothes. 'I am grey outside,' he said, 'but pure gold inside'. Though he ridiculed the courtiers who wore 'their mills and woods of tall trees on their backs'[3] (that is, who mortgaged their estates to buy lace and clothes for Court wear) he had few disciples of this idiosyncrasy. After his assassination in 1610, and the accession of his nine-year old son Louis XIII, Richelieu – Secretary of State but effectively in charge – encouraged the prodigality of the nobles, being set to ruin them financially, and so reduce their power. Only Marie de' Medici, nominally Regent, offspring of a middle-class banking family and money-conscious, attempted restraint, and in 1613 a law was passed prohibiting in particular 'the use of gold or silver, whether fine or counterfeit, and all lace of Milan, or of Milan fashion',[4] suggesting that Milanese laces at this time were far richer than the linen laces which later in the century bore their name.

The extravagance, however, was enormous. In that same year, in Britain, when James I's daughter Elizabeth married Frederick V, Elector Palatine and later King of Bohemia, the total cost was some £100,000, approximately equivalent to £3,500,000 today. In the surviving inventory of the wedding are listed, as well as numerous rich gowns: 1,698 oz of silver bone lace with spangles, and 667 oz of silver Myllen (Milan) bone lace, for the bride and, for the bridesmaids 338 lb 2 oz and a dram of broad and rich silver lace and loom lace.[5] Precious metals were quoted by weight rather than by length because of the importance of quality, that is the amount of silver which the thread, and therefore unit measurements of the lace, contained.

The silver ore came largely from Bohemia, while the partiality for gold laces was strongly linked with huge influxes from Spanish mines in the Americas, improvidently exploited by the Conquistadores. But the flooding of Europe with gold, so far from being advantageous, had had a recessionary effect, and Spain herself sank from immense prosperity to near-destitution, a process accelerated by Philip II's fatal wars such as the Armada against England which cost him 4,000 dead and over 80 galleons. During the reign of his son, Philip III, from 1598 to 1621, Spain's leadership of fashion waned, and for other countries the rigid ruffs and stiffly padded hose and farthingales began to give way to a softer line, as French fashions emerged into dominance.

Though ruffs changed their shape, and might be either strictly horizontal, or tilted up at the back and down at the front, or declining all round like a fading flower (fig. 21), the decoration of cutwork and punto in aria persisted; it was also during this quarter-century that bobbin, or bone, laces made of linen thread became of increasing importance in fashion. A portrait of Magdalena of Neuburg dated 1613 (fig. 22), shows a bouffant ruff with a lace around its gadrooned edges which is near-identical with those shown in woodcuts of bobbin lace patterns from Parasole's book printed in Rome in 1610 (fig. 23).

Other designs by Parasole appear in colour plate I, bordering the deeply scooped neckline of the bodice, while the translucent screen of silk or lawn stretched behind the head displays the needle lace punto in aria across its surface (see also fig. 24).

Similar low-cut bodices are shown in figs 25a and 26. In the first, Anne of Denmark wears a small flat

collar of black bobbin lace tied with tasselled strings. Though she had a reputation for extravagant dressing, the dark simplicity of this style suggests its association with a period of mourning, perhaps for her elder son, Henry Prince of Wales, who died in 1612 at the age of 18. Anne is known to have purchased English laces, and there is a homely naïvety about this ensemble which would support such an origin. Indeed the design is not altogether dissimilar from samples enclosed in the Isham letter of c.1625, and thought to have been made in Northamptonshire. Various State papers record laces bought in Hampshire, and Anne's patronage may have been important: four years after her death in 1619, the bone lace industry of Great Marlow, Buckinghamshire, was described as 'decayed', and the workers as in distress.[6]

In fig. 26 the bewitching Lady Digby shows how the falling ruff, so formally remote during the Spanish regime, could present quite a different aspect as it drooped softly, embroidered all over with cutwork, above a deep décolletage. She was 'a most beautiful desirable Creature,' wrote Aubrey.[7]

> She was sanguine and tractable and Richard, Earl of Dorset, made no delay to catch at such an opportunity. She had a most lovely and sweet turn'd face, the colour of her cheeks was just that of the Damaske rose. Sir Kenelme Digby [whom she married in 1625, and who was famous for his 'sympathetical powders prepared by Promethean fire'] had several pictures of her by Vandyke etc. Ben Jonson hath made her live in poetry, *Sitting, and ready to be drawne, What makes these Tiffany, silkes and lawne, Embroideries, feathers, fringes, lace, When every limbe takes like a Face!*

While men continued during the early years of the seventeenth century to wear much the same shapes and types of lace as women, the little turndown collar of the sixteenth century recurred (see fig. 13). Then it began to rise off the shoulders to form a brief horizontal shelf around the neck, known as the gollila, which needed either starch or, like the ruffs themselves, a wire support (fig. 27). This style, evanescent in England, persisted for men in Spain through the mid-century (see fig. 36) and even to 1700 when the Duke of Anjou, named by Charles II of Spain as his successor, entered Madrid to claim the throne as Philip V.

21 *The tilted falling ruff, chequered with cutwork and bordered with punto in aria. The black line crossing the ruff is a thin strand of plaited hair, extending from above the left ear, and known as a cadanette. Elizabeth of Bohemia, by Miereveldt, c.1623.*

22 *A billowing treble ruff bordered with bobbin lace, as are the non-matching cuffs. Compare fig. 23. Magdalena Herzogin, by Peter Candid, c.1613.*

23 *Designs from Parasole's pattern book, printed in Rome, 1610, from a nineteenth-century reprint.*

The siting of lace also sometimes varied between the sexes: while women wore lace on their heads, and exposed their chests, men exposed their legs and wore lace on their shoes and later around their knees, which women did not.

The shoe decorations, known as 'roses', were often of gold or silver lace since linen laces in such a position would be constantly begrimed. The lace was twisted into tight rosettes which sometimes swelled to an enormous size extending well beyond the width of the shoe until Mr Brooks M.P. in 1621 was heard complaining that gentlemen now spent more money on a pair of shoe roses than their fathers had spent on their entire wardrobe. An extreme price of £30 a pair was quoted.[8]

1625–1660

By 1625 the hold of Spain over fashion was past. Henrietta Maria, sister of Louis XIII, had married Charles I of Great Britain, and a transition into quite new styles had begun. Standing collars lowered themselves a little, to hover over the shoulders so that the broad laces around them projected outwards like feathered wings (fig. 28). At the same time falling ruffs, unstarched, sank lower, becoming 'confusion ruffs', which then collapsed around the neck and upper arms making tiered capes bordered with bobbin lace.

These falling collars, or whisks, were matched by upright cuffs, by close-fitting linen coifs worn by women and children, and by knee laces or canions (French, *canons*) worn by men. The laces which decorated them were made with bobbins, using an already traditional twisting and crossing technique. They were far superior to the heavy passements of the 1561 Zurich pattern book, and even to the more sophisticated Venetian laces of the brothers Sessa (1557).

The Parasole designs of 1610 had been delicate traceries made by the intersecting of plaited strands, probably near Genoa, and imitating the skeletal form of the then fashionable needle laces. The new scalloped laces, constructed from superb quality

24 *A close-up of a cuff showing that bobbin and needle laces can often be clearly distinguished in portraits,* *especially when they appear together. Detail from a portrait of Lady Bennet, c.1603.*

Flanders flax, were relatively thick and substantial, but of perfect smoothness, so that the firm cloth-work was as flat as if made by a master weaver. The closely segmented designs were peacefully pleasing, and had sometimes almost no openwork between them.

The style caught on throughout Europe, completely replacing needle laces in fashion, and is shown with marvellous clarity in portraits of Charles I by Van Dyck, Prince Matthias of Medici by Sustermans, Louis XIII by Pourbus, and King Christian IV of Denmark by Abraham Wuchters, as well as in enchanting engravings by Bosse (1602–76) and Hollar (1607–77) (figs 29, 30, 31).

Bourgeois styles might lag a little behind (fig. 32), but the almost instantaneous similarity of Court fashions throughout most of Europe was to some extent an effect of the extremely close inter-relationship between the royal families (see fig. 20). Marriages of first cousins abounded, and spouses were selected by a wish, or need, to consolidate territorial gains. Nor was it uncommon for kings to marry two, three or even four times, which extended their influence. Philip II, for example, had married in turn, between 1543 and 1570, Maria, daughter of the King of Portugal, Mary I of England, Elizabeth de Valois, sister of Henri III of France, and Anna of Austria, daughter of the Holy Roman Emperor Maximilian II.

While the general similarity of laces between these widely disseminated wearers is obvious, and the expected places of origin would be the commercial centres of Flanders and Genoa, both of which produced scalloped 'collar' laces in the first half of the seventeenth century, it is impossible, now, to tell with precision where any specific piece was made. There is plenty of evidence that English Devon laces copied Flemish styles, and that a similar practice existed in Denmark, but whether particular pieces were imported from Flanders, or made from Flemish prickings, or from rubbings of actual laces, or by expatriate Flemish workers, or by a pass-it-on method through the Catholic grapevine linking the convents of Europe, we do not know. King

25 *(a) Black bobbin lace, possibly English, worn by Anne of Denmark, c.1612. By Gheeraerts.*

(b) A dress banded all over with a simple black bobbin lace. Frances, Countess of Thanet. D. Mytens, c.1620.

Christian's famous collar, worn at the Battle of Kolberg-heide in 1644, is regarded as Danish in origin, and in 1647 he prohibited the importation of foreign laces as if Danish laces were now quite adequate for local fashion.

Though the line of clothes at this period might look almost plain and, after the excesses of the earlier years, quite pleasingly simple, the materials of which they were made remained fabulously expensive (fig. 33). Many sumptuary edicts were passed: one in 1633 placed such severe restrictions on collars, cuffs, lace, cutwork and embroideries of gold and silver that it occasioned engravings by Bosse in which French courtiers discard their finery

26 *A seductive version of the falling ruff, serving to emphasize the exposure of naked skin below. Lady Digby, by Isaac Oliver, c.1620.*

27 *The gollila. The stiffly floating collar is here decorated with needle lace, though it was sometimes worn quite plain. On his right knee James Hay wears a huge rosette, matching his frilled shoe roses. By George Geldorp, 1628.*

as if the very flesh was being torn from their bones.

The ineffectiveness of this, as of other edicts passed in 1634 and 1639, is shown by an inventory of the wardrobe of the Marquis de St Mars, Grand Master of the Stable to Louis XIV, after his death by beheading for treason in 1642, at the age of 22. The inventory included, among a vast number of items, a 'doublet of cloth of silver covered with black gauze, embroidered and slashed, lined with flesh-coloured satin, and bordered everywhere with Flanders lace'.[9] The enormous number of boot hose included in the inventory would certainly be lace-decorated, for when boots splayed out at the top, frills of lace overflowed from them as from a bucket of soap-suds.

In Britain, the many foolish prodigalities of James I piled up debts and unpopularity in massive proportions, and paved the way for his son's destruction on 30 January 1649, an event preceded by the Civil War. The romantic falling collars and cuffs, the sweeping feather-plumed hats and silk doublets, were the dress of Charles's supporters, the Royalists or Cavaliers (fig. 35). With Charles's

execution, and the exile of Henrietta Maria and her children to France and the haven provided by her nephew Louis XIV, the Roundheads or Parliamentarians took over under the Protectorate of Oliver Cromwell.

Though this, in theory, was a time when lace was banished from England, the Puritans were soon corrupted once a position of power was established. Colonel Hutchinson, instead of cropping his hair, wore it long as the Cavaliers did. General Harrison in 1650 appeared in the House of Commons in a scarlet cloak laden with gold and silver lace, and with every inch of his coat covered with cliquant, an adulteration of precious metal with copper.[10]

But someone had to suffer that puritanical ideals

28 *The collar refuses to settle, but juts outwards from the shoulders like partly opened wings, while a soft embroidered smock fills in the neckline. This was a particularly German fashion. Magdalena Sybille of Prussia, by Kilian, 1630.*

29 *The full, comfortable cut of this bright orange gown shows off the grey unbleached Flemish bobbin lace which lies flatly in two layers across the shoulders, matched by broadly spreading cuffs. Henrietta Maria, after Van Dyck, c.1632.*

30 *A neat tippet covers a more sedate collar, and a*
modest lace-trimmed smock leaves no inch of skin
exposed below the throat. Amsterdam school, 1640s.

Bosse In, et fé

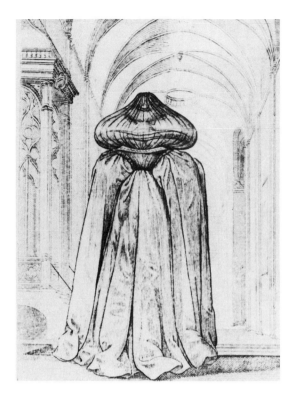

31 *(a) This low-situated collar is probably the out-turned neck of the smock, over which the stays are worn and the sleeves tied on, while the outer petticoat is hitched up for ease of walking. The face is protected by a veil of black gauze. By Bosse, c.1640. A similar engraving by Hollar bears the verse: 'In sumer when wee walke to take the ayre, We thus are Vayl'd to keep our faces faire, And lest our beautie should be soyl'd with sweate, We with our ayrie fannes depell the heate.'*

(b) A conch or conque, a gauze veil stretched like a fig-shaped balloon over a light metal frame. Worn mostly by widows, in France. Bosse, second quarter of the seventeenth century.

(c) A triangular tippet edged, like the low neckline and the cuffs, with scalloped Flemish bobbin lace, covers the bare shoulders, its casual disarray recalling Herrick's lines on Delight in Disorder, *written about 1650: 'A sweet disorder of the dress, Kindles in clothes a wantonness. A lawn about the shoulders thrown, Into a fine distraction [pronounced distrac-she-own]. An erring lace which here and there Enthrals the crimson stomacher. . . .' One of the 'Four Elements', 'Air', by Bosse.*

might be upheld, and it was the English lower classes, to which the bobbin lace-makers belonged, who were chosen to set an example by being deprived of all jollities. Restrictions became fanatical, until on 25 December of 1656 there was the first reading of a Bill for 'abolishing and taking away festivals, commonly called holydays', including Christmas Day itself.[11] It was small wonder that the people began to think nostalgically of the days of monarchy, and when Cromwell was buried in 1658 Evelyn wrote, 'It was the joyfullest funerale that ever I saw, for there were none that cried.'

1660–1680

In the year 1660 Charles II was declared King of Great Britain, and Louis XIV married Maria Theresa, daughter of Philip IV of Spain (fig. 37). Charles had been in exile in France and Flanders so that the influence on him of the Court of his first cousin, Louis XIV, was strong – though he had not the means to live richly. In May 1660 Pepys wrote: 'Mr Pickering told me in what a sad poor condition the King was, and all his attendants, their clothes not worth forty shillings the best of them. And how overjoyed the King was when Sir J. Greville brought him some money.'

Six months later Pepys was present himself at The Hague as Charles prepared to embark for England. There he met Charles's mother, Henrietta Maria, 'a very little plain old woman [she was 51]

32 *A millstone ruff decorated uncharacteristically with Flemish bobbin 'collar' lace. Petronella Buys, wife of a merchant and sea captain and Councillor of the Dutch East India Company. By Rembrandt, 1635.*

33 *(a) (opposite) Anne of Austria with the young Louis XIV, born 1638. She wears a dress of the richest turquoise silk woven with silver, and decorated with silver lace. The linen collar and cuffs appear here as separate accessories, not attached to the smock. The lace, conceivably made in Genoa, resembles the delightful patterns in Danieli's book published in Bologna in 1639 (fig. 33b – below).*

and nothing more in her presence in any respect nor garbe than any ordinary woman' (fig. 36). He also met Charles's aunt, the widowed Elizabeth of Bohemia whom he considered 'a very debonair but a plain lady'.

Charles was welcomed with great joy at Dover, and his procession to London was a triumphant one. Of his coronation on 22 April 1661, Pepys wrote, 'So glorious was the show, with gold and silver, that we were not able to look at it, our eyes being so much overcome.' It was quite natural that Charles should patronize the country he knew for the 'fine lawn, laced with fine Flanders lace' of his colobium sindonis,[12] and for his other coronation laces. For him, it was England that was unfamiliar territory.

34 *Shopping in the Galerie du Palais. Note that lace collars, gloves and fans can be bought 'off the peg', although really important pieces would still be commissioned. Women are bare-headed, or wear small black veils to protect their complexions. By Bosse, c.1650.*

As to the state of English lace-making at this time, especially the Devon-area laces which so closely resembled the non-continuous Brussels laces, we have no conclusive information. Thomas Fuller, writing at the time of the Restoration, though his work was only published posthumously in 1662, speaks of 'Honeyton lace' saving some thousands of pounds yearly, formerly sent overseas 'to fetch lace from Flanders',[13] but he makes no comment on its design, or quality, or the extent to which it constituted a lace acceptable to fashion.

Catherine, Charles's wife by proxy, had landed in Portsmouth in 1662, and some of her ladies-in-waiting went ahead of her to London: '... some Portugall ladys, which are come to towne before the Queene. They are not handsome,' Pepys commented, 'and their farthingales a strange dress.' The farthingale had disappeared in England some 30 years earlier, and Pepys at the age of 29 would not remember it.

The form of lace collar worn by Catherine in an engraving of her wedding, and in a portrait painted of her by Stoop, c.1662 (fig. 38), passes straight around her shoulders; in the portrait it rises high up on the neck, in the engraving it is low down off the shoulder. The transformation of the old falling collar into the bertha was simple, brought about merely by its falling a little lower so that it clung below the shoulder, vacillating between conceal-ment and indecent exposure. As shown in fig. 31c, the décolletage could be covered by a little tippet –

later known as a fichu or half-handkerchief – which was in effect very similar to the original falling collar except that it was V-shaped at the back instead of curved.

Close inspection of the portrait of Catherine shows that the lace of her bertha resembles neither a bobbin nor needle lace, but a buratto, like a Spanish *randas*, the woven gauze being either embroidered by hand, or the design itself manipulated on the loom, in the manner of loom laces (fig. 38c).

The change in women's clothes coincided with a change in men's. Doublets became short, revealing a voluminous shirt which billowed out at the waist

35 *(a) A scalloped Flemish bobbin lace of classic scrolling design embellishes the shirt of Endymion Porter, Royalist. The frill emerging through the unbuttoned doublet is a chitterling. By William Dobson, c.1645.*

(b) A later huntsman, in jacket instead of doublet; with a three-dimensional needle lace like Venetian gros point instead of Flemish bobbin; a wig instead of his natural hair; and an open shirt, his cravat left off, instead of a falling collar. By Nicolas de Largillière, c.1670.

over knee-length open-ended petticoat breeches. Flanked by long natural hair, or a wig, the collar was withdrawn from the shoulders where it would have been concealed by the hair, and concentrated in a narrow area below the chin where its lace assumed the richest possible form to compensate for the lack of space. Such a collar, broad at the front, and narrow along the back, was known as a rabat. Canions hung down from the knees, and matching cuffs stood upwards from the wrists.

The imposing grandeur of the baroque was now overtaking clothes. For a while the densely textured Dutch bobbin laces, made in the Antwerp area of Flanders and imported into the United Provinces, were displayed in many beautiful portraits of the period (figs 39, 40). But the most prestigious lace to emerge was a needle lace from Venice with great flowers filling superlative designs to give a magnificently sumptuous effect, though the work which made it was unbelievably fine, with thousands of buttonhole stitches crowded with exquisite precision into every particle of every bloom (fig. 44a). Though it remained in fashion until 1700, this superb lace, of a miraculous proficiency which

36 *The widowed Henrietta Maria in the long-outmoded falling collar of her youth, her head covered with a black veil. By P. de Champagne, c.1661.*

37 *The betrothal of Louis XIV and Maria Theresa, daughter of Philip IV of Spain, in 1660, on the Isle of Pheasants. The Spaniards are to the right, the French to the left, advancing towards each other with equal steps so that neither takes precedence over the other. The Spaniards are soberly dressed: Maria Theresa wears a farthingale, the men have ruffs and gollilas, long out of fashion in France and England. In contrast Louis XIV and his attendants overflow with ornament – ribbons everywhere, lace rabats, tiered cuffs, huge canons and elaborate shoe strings.*

38 *(a) Catherine of Braganza by D. Stoop, c.1662. Her elbows rest on the broad farthingale, and the rich silver lace of her petticoat can be seen at the side. The lace cuffs dome upwards, and the deep collar is a form of bertha.*

(b) Detail of the collar showing the appearance of a woven gauze.

(c) A loom lace, to show its comparable structure.

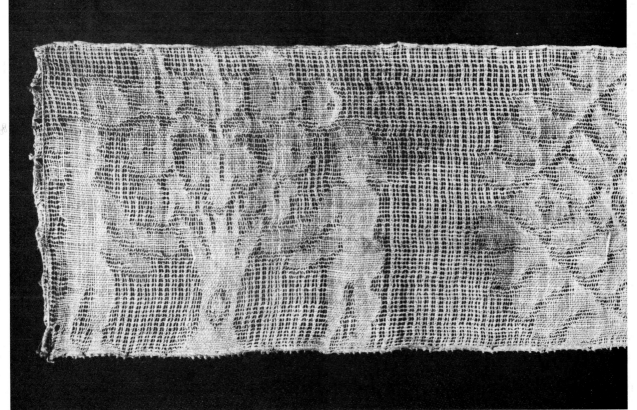

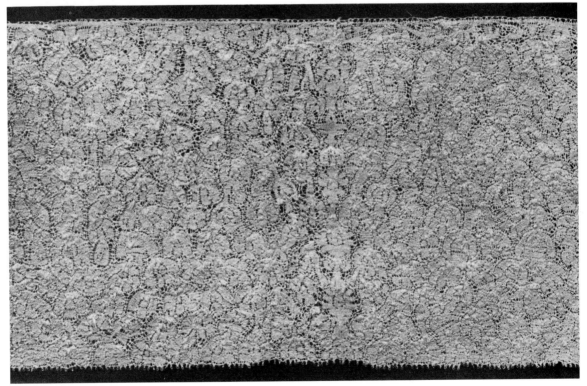

39 *(a) A densely compacted Dutch bobbin lace used to make elaborate cuffs arranged in three layers. Thought to be Anne Marie-Louise d'Orléans (1627–93), by P. Mignard.*
(b) Detail.
(c) An actual lace of this kind.

40 *An American portrait of Elizabeth Freake, of
Boston, with baby Mary, her eighth child. The emigrées
were avid for fashion, and dolls similar to those sent from
Paris to England also went to the Colonies. The sturdy
lace with its powerful Dutch design and clearly meshed
ground would have been imported from Flanders. Dutch
influence in New England was strong, Manhattan Island
having been bought by the Dutch in 1626, but ceded to the
English in 1664. Baby Mary's cap, collar and cuffs have
a simpler Antwerp (Anvers) lace. The gold and silver
work of Mrs Freake's skirt may be a gimp lace, or an
embroidery, and is East European in style, not unlike
the black lace in fig. 46. By an unknown artist, early
1670s.*

defies description, was a kind of Venetian swan-song as the ruined Republic sank from its heights of commercial splendour into insignificance, and the merchants of Venice lost their hold on the rich markets of France, England and Spain on which their livelihood depended.

Such grandeur could not but appeal to the youthful Louis XIV who, like the related Stuarts, was a staunch believer in the divine right of kings. Choosing the sun as his representative symbol, the Sun King was to write later in his memoirs:

> The sun, the most noble of all and which – by virtue of its unique quality, the brilliance which surrounds it, the light it gives to the other stars which behave as a Court to it, the good it achieves everywhere, creating joy and life on all sides by its perpetual motion – is without doubt the most vivid and beautiful image for a great King.[14]

Louis' financial excesses were early opposed by his mother Anne of Austria, as Regent, and by her Prime Minister and second husband, Mazarin. In 1660, with Louis on the verge of attaining in-dependent and personal rule, Mazarin shot his last bolt, a wordy compilation *Contre le Luxe* which attacked all luxurious dressing, and was intended to prohibit passements, guipures, embroideries, in fact all ornaments except the simplest silk ribbons. For liveried servants, wool was to be substituted for silk cloth, and was to be decorated by no more than two bands of braid or plain lace not more than an inch (*un pouce*) in width, and on the edges only. There were to be no laces of any kind imported from foreign lands, and 'canons' were not to be worn since they had become excessively rich, sometimes extending to three rows of frills. The resultant outcry was immense, avalanching into a long diatribe entitled *La Revolte des Passemens*, or the revolt of the laces against their imminent redundancy.[15]

In March 1661, when Mazarin died, all the cautionary proscriptions were overruled, and the crippling expenditure on bodily ornamentation accelerated again with lace ranking pretty high on the list of pecuniary haemorrhages.

Louis' new and very astute Controller General of Finance, Colbert, acting perhaps on the principle that if you can't beat them, join them, recognized at once that it was futile to ban lace since the Court was too firmly addicted and no one would benefit from the measure except smugglers. Instead Colbert planned, while prohibiting imported laces, to en-courage home manufacture. The result was the emergence of the points de France, made in pro-fessional establishments located at old lace-making

centres such as Arras, Sedan, Alençon and Aurillac, where women had long been skilled in the use of the needle, and where the now outdated cutworks had formerly been made. He had the sense to employ not only good designers but Venetian workers to instruct the natives so that within a short time a needle lace, at first imitative, but rapidly acquiring a character of its own, was ready to be marketed. Point de France continued to be worn to the end of the century, and is beautifully portrayed in portraits of Madame de Maintenon, and of the young Louise, daughter of the exiled James II and his second wife Mary of Modena (see fig. 133).

Similar French attempts in the area of bobbin laces failed dismally, for Flemish bobbin laces had, during the mid-century, been developing into the most amazing fabrics of an incredible lightness, beauty and complexity of design, needing often more than a thousand bobbins, and a thread so slender that the slightest gaucheness of handling would snap it in pieces. There was no way that French bobbin laces, still for the most part of a stout peasant type, could compete with these aery ghosts.

Flemish bobbin laces were thus at this time achieving a position where they had no serious rival. The bobbin laces of Genoa and Milan had suffered from the stultifying effect of Spanish domination. Genoa had progressed little beyond its earlier scalloped form, and both areas were still

41 *An affidavit of the Burial in Woollen Act.*

42 *The beginning of the fashion for breeches and ribbons, in France, c.1650–60. On the left, canons emerge from the boot tops.*

producing passements of gold, silver and coloured silks so rich that their importation was repeatedly prohibited. Genoese laces, in fact, almost died out in 1678 when Louis XIV in martial mood bombarded the city and forced the Doge to kneel before him at Versailles. Thereafter Genoa's linen laces appear to have been made only for church use.

Gold and silver laces continued to be in demand for more splendid occasions. Colour plate 2 shows the Holy Roman Emperor Leopold I of Austria (whose first wife was Margaret Theresa, half-sister

of Louis XIV's wife Maria Theresa) reclining languidly against a stone plinth 'dressed as a shepherd'. He is of course no mortal shepherd but the divinely singing Tircis of Virgil's *Bucolica*, a favourite of the popular and lavishly magnificent Court masques. His doublet is richly decorated with gold lace, and extraneous wings of lace sprout from his elbows.

In England, Charles II's nationalistic efforts at economy were a good deal less successful than those of Louis. In 1662 Charles passed an Act prohibiting the importation of foreign bone laces, cutworks etc, on the grounds that there was a very adequate home industry which not only supplied the kingdom but provided revenue through the duties on the imported thread required for its manufacture. He did not, however, rate it so highly as to wear it himself, and in 1668 there was a plea from Parliament:

> This House doth humbly desire his Majesty that by his own example, and his Queen's, and the Duke's and the Duchess's [of York], he will be pleased forthwith to encourage the wearing of his own English manufactures, and to discourage the wearing of all foreign manufactures. Resolved: that this House will begin themselves to show a good example herein unto the Nation.[16]

Meanwhile, the Duchess of York, wife of the future James II, kept determinedly to £5,000 a year for her own spending at a time when a common soldier was paid £14 per annum, and £8 was regarded as a very adequate wage for a good servant.[17]

One effort of the King's which did eventually succeed was the promotion of the English woollen trade, which was still of great importance to the country's economy. To this end he introduced the Burial in Woollen Act of 9 January 1666–7.* It was extremely unpopular, and at first unsuccessful, but it was renewed with greater success in 1678.[18] Burial may seem a strange occasion for high fashion, but the vanity of courtiers by no means ended with their last breath. They planned ahead to the pomp and ceremony of their funeral, determined to go to earth in their best clothes, though whether to impress the mourners or their Maker is hard to tell.

Charles's law was primarily directed against the importation of Dutch and French linens which were strong favourites for shrouds. Since the death rate was high, and corpses plentiful, a considerable amount of money was involved, some £150,000 per annum. In August 1665, at the height of the plague, deaths in London alone had averaged well over 3,000 a week. To enforce the law a declaration had to be sworn at each funeral that nothing but wool had been used. Fig. 41 shows one such declaration, issued in 1705. It reads:

> George Winn of the parish of St Bartholomews in the City of London, maketh oath that Mary Willcox, an infant ... lately deceased, was not put in, wrapt or wound up or buried in any shirt, shift, sheet or shroud made or mingled with flax, hemp, silk, hair, gold or silver, or other than what is made of sheep's wool only, nor in any coffin lined or faced with any cloth, stuff, or any other thing ... dated the 27th day of July in the fourth year of the reign of our sovereign Lady Anne, by

* In the seventeenth century, Britain was still using the Roman, or Julian, calendar, although most other countries in Europe used the Gregorian. Julian dates were ten days behind Gregorian, thus 9 January would be 1666 in Britain, 1667 elsewhere.

the grace of God of England, Scotland, France and Ireland Queen, Defender of the Faith etc, and in the year of our Lord God, 1705.

The connection of this Act with lace lies in the granting of a monopoly for the making of woollen laces for burying the dead to Amy Potter of St Paul's Churchyard, a shopping centre, on 4 October 1678. The patent (No. 204) reads: 'Potter, Amy. An invenĉon for makeing of Flanders Colbertine and all other laces of woollen, to be used in and about the adorneing or makeing-up of dresses and other things for the decent burial of the dead or otherwise.' Colberteen is thus confirmed as a coarse woollen lace, made with bobbins, 'an inferior lace for everyday wear', as was in fact suggested by reports of travellers at that time, and by references to it in Congreve and Swift.

Indeed, English laces as a whole at this period might well be more relevant to Chapter 8, Peasant Laces, for their praises, though not lacking, are sparsely sung. Surviving needle laces are for the most part heavy and inelegant, except for hollie point (page 120), and they were probably utilitarian or ecclesiastical rather than fashionable in the accepted sense. A patent (No. 182) of 1645, granted

43 *The snowball ground of this rabat is pure Flanders, the wormlike coils East European, suggesting an Austrian influence. By J. A. Eismann, 1668.*

44 *(a) A cravat of Venetian gros point mounted on a ribbon which ties at the back of the neck. The Grand Condé, Duc de Bourbon, and his son. By Claude Lefebvre, c.1668.*

(b) (below) A cravat end of the needle lace known as point de Sedan. The sumptuous Oriental design encloses an amazing variety of buttonhole stitches. 1670s. (Sedan was captured by the French in 1642.)

45 *(opposite) 'La manière que les François son habillé soubs le regne de Louis XIII en 1671 1. Les Mains dans les poche et les gants sous le bras . . . 3. la mode des ringrave . . .' French fashions of 1671. The rhingraves (petticoat-breeches) are worn with the new Persian-style coat, left open at the front to show the shirt frill, and a lace rabat with two sets of tassels. The 'bands in the pockets, and gloves under the arm' go along with the coat; the earlier doublets were too short for bands to go into them. The woman's dress also shows a new style, the mantua, with the laced chemise visible below short sleeves, and the open skirt drawn back to reveal the petticoat. A translucent tippet fits closely around the shoulders and lace bertha.*

to William Fanshawe, Gabriel Cox and Rebecca Croxton, was for 'Working and Waveing of point laces after the manner of point de Venise and point de Espayne'. The wording is obscure, and though one might guess that needle laces similar to Venetian gros point – then in its early days – must be intended, it leaves the inclusion of two male names, and the word 'waveing' (weaving) unexplained. Both were associated with Stocking Frame and bobbin lace work, but not usually with needle laces.

It appears that Charles, in addition to restricting the importation of linen laces, attempted like Mazarin to restrict the wearing of those of gold and silver, in 1662. For while Pepys in 1661 views with dismay the 'gold laced suit' of Captain Holmes, fearing he has dastardly designs upon his wife, he makes no other comment. In May 1662, however,

Pepys sees 'the King in a suit laced with gold and silver which it is said was out of fashion'; and in 1664, 'To the Park and there met the Queene coming from Chapell, with her Maids of Honour, all in silver-lace gowns again, which is new to me and that which I did not think would have been brought up again.' A year later the situation has changed, and Pepys himself is forsaking his customary black suit for 'a new coloured-silk suit and coat trimmed with gold buttons and gold broad lace round my hands, very rich and fine.'

Accounts for haberdashery from Mrs Woodreff, Milliner, in 1665, list gold and silver laces at 4s 4d an ounce; and similar accounts name silver bone lace at 6s a yard, black Flanders lace (see fig. 46) varying in price from 11½d to 3s 4d a yard, gold and silver cheine (chain-stitch) at 5s 6d, and the intriguing

46 *The long-waisted bodice, the short sleeves, and the full skirt caught back from a richly encrusted petticoat, are all trimmed with a black bobbin lace exquisitely rendered so that every detail of the pinnate fronds coiled through the reseaud ground is clearly seen. Similarly the flat white lace, with its sinuous foliage and decorative ground, is startlingly clear. The cuffs are attached to the full-sleeved smock. Geertruida den Dubbelde, by Bartholomeus van der Helste, 1668.*

silver Curle, black loome foote, broad loome lace, and white gimpe French lace at 4s.[19] Where there is no mention of another country it is reasonable – but no more – to assume that the laces may have been made in England. (12d = 1s = 5p.)

The form of dress in this Restoration period is often described as foolishly and recklessly extravagant, but so it had been for nearly a century, and so it was to remain for some decades more. It was, however, rather the courtiers and the aspirants who thus ruined themselves in their struggle for advancement: kings and queens were often markedly indifferent to sartorial glory. Quite simply they did not need it. Clothes magnified the person: the royal personage was already larger than life.

Petticoat breeches with 'as much ribbon as would have plundered six shops and set up twenty country Pedlars, and all the body drest like a May Pole' were a French fashion turning the English into 'forreign Butterflies', according to Evelyn.[20] But plain breeches remained for bureaucratic wear: Pepys, June 1665, 'Up, and put on my new stuff suit with close [not open like petticoat breeches] knees. At noon put on my first laced-band, all lace . . . to the Old Exchange and bought two lace bands more.' This band, or collar, was presumably a rabat (fig. 43). As wigs became longer, hiding much of the band, Pepys wondered, 'What will be the fashion after the plague is done as to periwigs, for nobody will dare to buy any hair for fear of the infection, that it had been cut off the heads of people dead of the plague?'

The Persian-style coat or justaucorps was introduced for Court wear by Charles II in October 1666, to replace the short doublet, at a time of enmity with the French who had joined forces with the Danes to support the Dutch in their war against England. It had no collar, but buttoned high to the base of the neck, so that a rabat could not easily be worn with it, and it therefore over a period of time came to be

47 *(a) The deshabillé look. Louise de Kéroualle, Breton maid of honour to Henrietta, Duchess of Orléans, and mistress of Henrietta's brother, Charles II. She became the Duchess of Portsmouth. 'She was for the most part in her undress all day,' wrote Evelyn. The lace on her smock is point de France. By Henri Gascars, c.1682.*

(b) Venetian gros point trims the very low neck, front opening and sleeves of the smock, which is partly covered by a blue mantle. Sophie Dorothea and her children – the future George II, and his sister Sophia. By an unknown artist, 1689.

replaced by the linen cravat, knotted at the throat in such a way that it displayed broad ends of lace beneath the chin (fig. 44). This English fashion of coat, breeches, cravat and vest (waistcoat) was not formally adopted by the French Court until nearly ten years later (fig. 45).

Women's gowns between 1625 and 1660 had been flowing, high-waisted and with full sleeves and cape-like falling collars fastened either around the throat, or exposing a larger or smaller amount of bare shoulder and breast. After 1660, perhaps influenced by the queens from Spain and Portugal, tight-lacing returned, bodices became décolleté and long-waisted, and skirts were opened, exposing a petticoat often lavishly decorated like those made immortal by Pepys, writing on 21 May 1662: 'In the Privy-garden I saw the finest smocks and linnen petticoats of my Lady Castlemain [Barbara Villiers, a mistress of the King, cousin of the second Duke of Buckingham, and later Duchess of Cleveland] laced with rich lace at the bottom that ever I saw: and did me good to look at them.' These in fact were real undergarments (see page 134), washed and spread in the White Hall Palace grounds, to dry in everyone's view, on the very day of the wedding of Charles to the luckless Catherine of Braganza. It was a completely literal washing of dirty linen in public.

A further licentiousness was added to the Restoration atmosphere by the innovation of the negligée or deshabille look, popularized in England by the paintings of Lely which were, said Pepys, 'good, but not like'. This uninhibited style of dress, also known as the nightgown or morning gown, appealed to him, and he noted approvingly that the actress Knipp 'came out in her nightgowne with no lockes [no false curls] and which is the comeliest dress that ever I saw her in', and 'Lady Castlemain

Dame travaillant en Tapisserie.

Cette Belle n'est point oisive,   Mais la main n'est guere attentive,
Son ouurage et Tircis l'occupent tour a tour: Quand le cœur et l'esprit ne Songent qu'a l'amour
                    Paris, Chez Bonnart ruë S.t Iacques, au Coq, auec priuil.

48 *Steinkirks are worn looped up through a buttonhole, and lace-ended. The tall fontange has a cap back and lappets, the ruffles are full and 'weeping'. The sleeves of the gown have been removed, leaving the smock visible beneath a corseted bodice belted at the waist over an open, trained skirt. In this and fig. 156, note the patches on their faces, the uniformity of 'the soft and childish features of the day', as Michelet called them: 'This childishness, so devoid of innocence, combined with the masculine Steinkirk, gives them the appearance of pages who have stolen women's garments.' The admirer – Tircis in the verse below – wears the justaucorps over a long vest and knee-length breeches. By Bonnart, 1693.*

ran out in her smock [shift or chemise], looking into White Hall garden, and thither her woman brought her her nightgown'. This was written in 1667, but Pepys was already making use of the fashion for his amorous deceits. On 4 December 1665, he was persuading Mrs Penington to 'undress her head and sit dishevelled all night'; by 20 December he was praying her 'to undress herself into her nightgown' that he 'might see how to have her picture drawn carelessly', that is in deshabille. This informality became a habit of men too: July 1665, 'Up and in my nightgown, cap and neckcloth, undressed all day', he says.

1680–1700

These so-called nightgowns were not for sleeping in. They were instead intended as semi-simple robes for relaxation. They had little lace themselves, but the lace decoration of the shirts and smocks beneath was left clearly visible (fig. 47). For women, the nightgown was already developing a more formal version, known as the mantle, or mantua, a term first used in this sense in the 1680s. Cut in one piece, and shaped something like a university gown, with short cuffed sleeves and an open front, the skirt was drawn back in a variety of ways to expose a rich petticoat (see fig. 49). Small aprons of lace were sometimes worn over them, and gloves or mittens too might be made of lace. These fashions are shown in many French engravings of the last two decades, such as those by Jean de St Jean, Nicolas Arnaud, Bonnart and Berain.

Three new feminine modes of wearing lace were introduced at this period: the fontange, the flounce and the steinkirk. The steinkirk was, according to one story, an impromptu side-effect of war when in 1692 the forces of the Grand Alliance under William III and the Duke of Marlborough attempted to surprise the forces of France under the Duke of Luxembourg, near the Flemish village of Steenkerke in the province of Hainault – of which Valenciennes was the capital. The French princes had no time for the ritualistic knotting of their cravats, and had to thrust them hurriedly through the button loops of their tunics. They were ultimately victorious, at the cost of over 16,000 dead or wounded on the two sides. The careless yet studied look of the Steenkerk, or Steinkirk, cravat was admirably in keeping with the casual notions of the times. Worn initially by men, the style was very soon adopted by women (fig. 48).

In France, cravats and steinkirks were garnished with point de France, the official lace of Court. In England Venetian gros point, as magnificent as ever, was favoured by the remaining Stuarts. A cravat of this lace was ordered by James II for his coronation in 1685, costing him £36.[21]

Flounces might take the form of one deep piece, or of a series of narrower bands. They might be of a variety of laces, and from contemporary illustrations it is not always easy to decide their geographical source (fig. 49). In addition, black and white engravings which appear to show lace may not in fact do so. Lace designs were used for embroidered or brocaded silks, and vice versa,[22] and were even printed on linen and cotton fabrics: 'went with my wife to the New Exchange where we saw some new fashion pettycoats of sarcenett [a plain weave silk with a finer weft] with a broad black lace printed

49 *The flounce. The petticoat, revealed by the lifted skirt, is banded with lace, probably point de France. The square neck of the gown has a lace tucker, the open bodice is laced like stays, and the elbow-length sleeves have flowing engageants. The whole is shrouded in a mantle of transparent gauze patterned with small flowers. The fontange points forward, and the edge of the cap back and lappets can be seen. Madame la Duchesse de Roquelaire* en habit d'este *(summer fashion), 1695.*

round the bottom and before, very handsome'.[23] 'Before' presumably means down the front of the petticoat where it was framed by the open skirt.

The fontange, like the steinkirk, was an innovation of the French, but a more romantic one. Marie-Angélique de Scoraille de Rousille became in 1678, at the age of 17, Maid of Honour to Henrietta, Duchess of Orléans, a sister of Charles II. Described by Madame de Sévigné as 'the most beautiful woman at Court', Marie-Angélique set her sights on Louis XIV, determined to oust his long-established favourite Madame de Montespan, herself beautiful, who had appeared in 1676 'entirely dressed in point de France, her hair in a thousand curls, hung with black ribbons, pearls and diamonds.' By the spring of 1679 Marie-Angélique had gained her objective, and though the subsequent birth of a still-born baby ruined her health and resulted in recurrent haemorrhages, she re-

turned to favour. On 6 April 1680, Madame de Sévigné wrote, 'Madame de Fontanges is a duchess with a pension of 20,000 ecus [see page 155]. Today she received compliments, in her bed [a favourite venue for social gatherings], and the king himself was there publicly. Tomorrow she takes her tabouret.' The tabouret was a very special favour, a small round stool which permitted the possessor to sit in the presence of the king. It was granted only to duchesses, foreign princesses, and Princesses of the Blood i.e. directly related to Louis, everyone else having to stand. However her ill-health made her 'eternally sad' and by September 1680 'the king's fire was extinguished'.[24] Ten months later she was dead.

Meanwhile she had started a new fashion for the head, an area which for ladies had remained largely uncovered since the 1640s when the coifs trimmed with scalloped Flemish laces went out of fashion. Said to have developed from a new way of tying up the hair, the fontange originated during Marie-Angélique's period of favour, caught on, and soon became extremely elaborate as the ladies of Court fought to outdo each other in splendour.

At its peak it consisted of a built-up hairstyle topped by a tower of lace supported by wire and subtended by a pair of lappets or streamers which denoted by their length the lady's rank. They were at first broad (fig. 50), but later narrowed, with a separate cap back or crown (fig. 156). It was essentially a Court fashion and as such attracted all the magnificence and perfection of which lace-makers were capable. It was in these fontanges that the bobbin laces of Flanders reached their supreme form in delicacy, design and execution. In spite of all the import restrictions some two million livres, or over £90,000 of Flemish lace entered France in 1681 (Paulis).

The precise significance of the term 'Flanders lace' in the seventeenth century is perhaps unfathomable. Even the geographical area encompassed by Flanders has all the vacillating indeterminateness of a mirage. Dominated by Spain, then by the Austrian Habsburgs, then after the death of the childless Isabella in 1633 by Spain once more, invaded repeatedly by Louis XIV until in 1683 Evelyn wrote despairingly that the French had 'almost swallowed' all Flanders, it would seem impossible to attribute to it any distinctively national features.

Yet its production of immense quantities of laces of exquisite beauty is irrefutable, being established by hundreds of documentary references, portraits, and surviving pieces of lace. We even have the names of areas where the laces were made, for in

50 *Queen Mary II. The tucker and stand-out ruffles of her smock show beyond the neckline and short sleeves of her silk mantua. The fontange or commode is raised in three tiers supported by wire. The lappets are long and broad, giving the whole something of the appearance of a mantilla. The lace is point de France, which Mary brought to England with her in 1688, at the end of her exile. By J. Smith after Vandervaart, c.1689.*

Louis' preparations for home production in 1664 he lists tariffs to be imposed on imported laces from Brussels, Mechlin, Antwerp, Liège, Louvain, Binche, Bruges, Ghent, Ypres and Courtray.[25] There is, however, no guidance at all as to their differences in technique or design; in short we are not told how one can be distinguished from another.

The amazing fineness of Flemish laces as early as 1651 is described in a Latin verse written by 'Jacobi Eyckii' and published in Antwerp. He gives an evocative description of its texture: 'this web is of the lightness of a feather, which in its price is too heavy for our purses'. His verbal image of the lace-maker 'seated at work in her Brabantine home' will be recognized at once by all bobbin lace makers:

> She flashes the smooth balls and thousand threads into the circle. Often she fastens with her hand the innumerable needles [pins] to bring out the various figures of the pattern; often, again, she unfastens them.

The issue is a fine web, open to the air with many an aperture, which feeds the pride of the whole globe, and shows grandly round the throats and hands of kings.[26]

The thousands of balls (round-ended bobbins) and threads indicate a continuous lace where cloth-work design and openwork ground are formed by the same threads. Non-continuous laces, made as separate particles of design each constructed from its own set of threads, need relatively few bobbins since each piece, as it is made, is quite small. The particles are attached to each other, or to a ground, by a process of 'taking sewings' which involves drawing minute threads through almost invisible loops using a tiny needle or hook. The vast number of attached threads may then be worked with bobbins, a few at a time, until all the spaces between are filled with openwork.

Such non-continuous laces are now attributed to the area around Brussels. They have a distinctive appearance and, in their delicate way, a very rich design. They appear to have been marketed under the trade name *point d'Angleterre* from about 1680, and this term occurs over and over again in French accounts, and in some engravings, of the late seventeenth century. Their relation to the laces described as *dentelle d'Angleterre* and *dentelle façon d'Angleterre* is obscure. Both are mentioned in the *Revolte des Passemens* of 1661 and, in a letter of Madame de Sévigné written on 6 November 1676, explaining the new fashion for 'transparents', she says: 'These are entire gowns of the most beautiful gold and blue brocades that one could see, and over them are worn mantles [manteaux] of black gauze or of beautiful *dentelle d'Angleterre*.'

Such fine Flemish thread as that described by Eyckii would certainly have been used not only for Flemish bobbin laces but also for the consummate Venetian gros points with their microscopic perfection of needle lace stitches (see page 39).

The closing years of the seventeenth century saw a megalomaniac tendency in Louis XIV, forcing courtiers to bankrupt themselves in order to appear worthy to be seen in his presence, and the nobility decimated by endless wars intended to establish forever France's mastery over Europe. In such a society it was only the suppliers who flourished: the suppliers of weapons for battle, of fabrics for dress, of money to tourniquet the financial wounds, and of that love which grasped at titles and fortunes for its many offspring. Ceaselessly a new nobility and a new rich were growing over and erasing the old until the whole structure of society was transformed, with the introduction of mercenary values which were ultimately to bring about the downfall of kings (fig. 156).

3

The Eighteenth Century

A PERIOD OF TRANSITION

1700–1750

The eighteenth century had an ambience which differed markedly from that of the previous 100 years. The distinction might broadly be encompassed by the terms baroque and rococo. The seventeenth century had been grandly extrovert; laces excelled themselves in their superhuman closeness of workmanship, both in the tiered and sculptured needle forms, and in those bobbin whispers of closely packed, almost invisible threads floating from the pillow like a complex web of gossamer.

The eighteenth century on the other hand was to be an age of scepticism and unrestricted thought, almost of flights of ideas, when both metaphysics and empiricism captured an open-minded enthusiasm. The founding of the Royal Society by Charles II, and the urge to experiment which had accompanied it, encouraged a freshness of approach which could question everything from the nature of fire – 'how it goes out in a place where the ayre is not free' (Pepys 1665) – to the divine right of kings. In such an atmosphere it became apparent that the glittering world which teemed with lace was no more than a tiny segment of the world of people.

In Britain by 1700 the doom-laden daughters of James II were bringing the reign of the Stuarts to a final close. Mary II had died of smallpox in 1694, at the age of 32. Her sister Anne, plagued with gout and saddened by her many dead babies, had little heart for the inconsequences of fashion, though Mechlin lace was a close favourite.

In France, the ageing Louis XIV grew sombre under the censorious influence of his second wife, Madame de Maintenon, whom he had married in 1684. From the glorious splendour he had so assiduously cultivated through his near-70 years as king, little remained. France's national debt stood at millions of pounds. The *Spectator*, with the cool rationality of the times, calculated in 1711 that in 20 years of French battles, Louis had squandered the lives of 800,000 of his male subjects, driven away

some 400,000 of his reformed subjects (Protestants or Huguenots), and gained as a result no more than a small area of Habsburg land – part of west Flanders – with a total population of not more than 250,000.

During the War of the Spanish Succession (1700–13), with Holland and England backing the claim of the Holy Roman Emperor Leopold I of Austria (colour plate 2) to the Spanish throne against an alliance of France, Spain and Bavaria backing Philip d'Anjou, many of the battles took place on the ground of Flanders, or the Spanish Netherlands. Of the precious lace-making centres there, all the more westerly – Lille, Valenciennes, Tournai, Bruges, Aresnes, Arras and Mons – were at various times fought over, which could not but affect their production. The more easterly cities of Brussels, Ghent, Antwerp and Mechelen, though further removed from the war, suffered in common with the whole of Flanders an even more deadly effect, the loss of trade.

Lace for Flanders was a commercial commodity, made for export. In spite of prohibitions based on its ruinous expense, its market had been the whole of Europe. The import restrictions against it had been easily made nonsense of by smugglers with a hundred ingenious ploys to fool the Customs men. It even became the fashion in England for ladies to desire only what was prohibited, and laces and linens were easily passed by Flemish merchants to Dutch traders, and so across the Channel.

Illicit interference with the trade to America had more disastrous effects. Spanish vessels laden with Flemish laces for the colonies in Chile and Peru were attacked by English and Dutch vessels which pirated the cargoes and diverted them to New England and Virginia. Vessels belonging to the French enemy were similarly treated. In March 1704 the *Boston News Letter* recorded: 'A Privateer sloop called the *Sea Flower* was cast away and broke in pieces, by a violent Easterlie storm, being bound from Curaçoa to Rhode Island with divers prize goods, viz. a parcel of Flanders lace of divers sorts

51 *The Spectator's 'enormous concave'. The little flat lace cap has its lappets pinned up; small frills of lace emerge below the cuffs; and a patterned tippet is knotted at the neck. 'The Reading Party', by Jean François de Troy, c.1730.*

in two great sea chests, taken from the Spaniards and French in the Spanish West Indies'. The cargoes of pirated ships were put up for public sale: 'On Wednesday next will be exposed for sale the ship *San Francisco* and her lading, taken by Capt. Rouse of Her Majesty's [Queen Anne's] ship *Sapphire*, consisting of all sorts of gold and silver lace, bone lace, Gympt lace, Black lace ...'. That these were fashion laces, and avidly sought after, is indicated by notices of theft, many of which specify Flanders: 'Stolen or carried away out of the house of Capt.

John Bonner in Cow Lane, 3 laced Head-dresses [commodes], 2 laced handkerchieves, 3 pr of laced sleeves.'[1]

Indeed, the battles over the Spanish Netherlands at this period have been called the Lace Wars. Every participant wanted the rich revenues which this commodity represented. But they wanted them without paying for them. Flanders, at the peak of its artistic blossoming, with a buoyant creative spirit excelling in glorious design, was suddenly in danger of being starved of that income without which any further production would be impossible.

The laces of north Italy were even more endangered. Milanese laces, so rich in the seventeenth century that they were the object of recurrent sumptuary edicts, floundered under the reactionary rule of the Spanish Habsburgs. In 1700, when Milan was invaded by Leopold and his Austrian army, the market to France and Spain, both enemies in the current war, was lost, and its era of fashion at an end.

Venice was in the death throes of its suicidal wars against the Turks, which lasted from 1684 to 1718, leaving her broken and unproductive, all her Aegean possessions lost, shrunk territorially and financially almost to insignificance, unable to adapt to any new trends in fashion, as her superb baroque laces became outmoded.

Thus, right at the beginning of the century lace in fashion suffered the most appalling setbacks – and ones due to external factors rather than to fashion's innate fickleness. Venice and Milan played no further definitive part in lace fashion. The influence of Genoa had ended in 1678 (page 46). France, bankrupted to such an extent that the nobility were ordered to melt down their antique silver platters and eat off 'clay' in order to finance the war, ended her point de France. The compulsory magnificence of Court life was in abeyance. In Flanders the lace trade was depressed. In Britain, never a major commercial producer, yet remote from the actual fields of battle, lace production continued. Honiton and Dorset laces, praised by Dr Yonge in 1702, and by the inventive Daniel Defoe in 1724, may have sought to replace the Flemish laces, but of their appearance or the part they played in fashion at this time we have little factual knowledge.

Through a suspension of inventiveness, the main fashions in clothes showed no immediate changes. Commodes, or fontanges, though now a little lower than before, and tilted forwards instead of bolt upright, still dominated the heads of women, and cravats the necks of men. Yet as the economic situation of all countries worsened there soon developed the strangest state of affairs in which lace, so prolifically flourishing at the end of the seventeenth century, was suddenly absent. Addison in June 1711 was mocking those 'wonderful Structures of Ribbands, Bone-lace and Wire' raised by 'Female Architects'. They are part of a 'Redundance of Excrescences' needing to be 'pruned very frequently'. In 1712, however, he was delighted to report that 'Ladies have been for some time in a kind of *moulting season*, having cast great quantities of Ribbon, Lace and Cambrick' so that their 'antiquated Commodes' were now replaced by the 'prettiest coloured hoods' on which he could gaze down, at the Opera, as upon a 'bed of tulips'.

From his writings, the end of the fontange began in July 1711: 'Their petticoats are now blown up into a most enormous Concave. Their superfluity of ornaments seem only fallen from their Heads upon

52 *A separate cap comprising a teacosy-shaped back, and an edge frill continuous with the lappets. Here the lace is Alençon, but many were made of Flemish bobbin laces.*

their lower Parts' (fig. 51). Looking at a sixteenth-century portrait he jibes: 'My great great great grandmother has on the new fashioned petticoat, except that the modern is gathered at the Waste. My Grandmother appears as if she stood on a large Drum whereas the Ladies now walk as if they were in a go-cart'. This interesting comparison of inflated skirts, over 100 years apart, compares the French farthingale of *c.*1600 (see fig. 14) with the huge volante of *c.*1710, spread over a hooped petticoat and reaching to the ground so that the movements of the feet could not be seen. The go-cart (see fig. 127) was a triangular baby-walker with wheels at the corners, and such a structure was in fact used in some European folk dances where the dancers supported themselves on it, keeping their feet off the floor, so that they indeed glided, with an astonishing smoothness.

During the same period, the continuing enmity between France and England, with France ready to support the Jacobite rebellion of 1715, caused a

(a)

(b)

divergence in fashion, away from the dominance of the French Court. The new English fashions were described in the *Spectator* of 28 July 1711, and the terrible ostracism lying in wait for those who dragged behind was pointedly made clear. A sensation was created by the Lady of the Manor, returning from a visit to London, as she entered her local church in the latest mode: 'Some stared at the prodigious bottom, and some at the little top, of this strange dress', the locals all being 'so far behind the times to appear as if from Charles II's reign'. 'At Salisbury,' the narrator continues spitefully, the wife of a Justice of the Peace was 'at least ten years behindhand in her Dress. She was flounced and furbelowed from head to foot, every Ribbon was wrinkled and every Part of her Garments in Curl, so that she looked like one of those Animals which in the Country we call a Freezeland Hen.' 'Steinkirks' he goes on, 'have just reached Newcastle', the fashion having started in France 20 years before (see

53 *(a) A typical design of Dresden work embroidered on muslin.*

(b) Drawnwork in the making. The pattern is outlined on glazed cotton, over which the woven fabric is fixed. A fine mesh has been created by a counted thread technique, leaving the flowers composed of the original cloth. The design strongly resembles some in the Danish pattern book of 1760.

(c) Drawnwork imitating a Brussels bobbin lace. The edges of the flowers and leaves have been strengthened with stem stitch to give the appearance of raised work (compare colour plate 3). Probably English, mid-eighteenth century.

page 52), and there are 'several Commodes in those parts which are worth taking a Journey thither to see' – meaning presumably that they were still extremely high.

Yet such dress remained the fashion in France. 'Before our correspondence with France was un- happily interrupted by the War,' writes Budgell in the *Spectator* of 17 January 1712, 'our Ladies had all their Fashions from thence; which the Milliners took Care to furnish them with by Means of a jointed Baby, that came regularly over, once a Month, habited after the manner of the most eminent Toasts [Society ladies] in Paris.' He speaks of their efforts 'even in the hottest Time of the War' to import the 'wooden Mademoiselle'. A lady writes at the same time: 'I have long bewailed, in Secret, the Calamities of my Sex during the War, in all which Time we have laboured under the insupport- able Inventions of English tire-women [dress- makers], who, tho' they sometimes copy indiffer- ently well, can never compose with the *Gout* they do in *France*.' When eventually a 'dear Moppet' was somehow brought over, and the lady managed at last to see it: 'You can imagine how ridiculously I

find we have all been trussed up during the War, and how infinitely the French Dress excells ours. The Mantua has no Leads [weights] in the sleeves; the Petticoat has no whalebone, but sits with an air altogether gallant and dégagé; the coiffure is in- expressibly pretty....'

When Mr Budgell himself saw the 'Puppet' he was less agreeably impressed. It was dressed in a

Cherry-coloured Gown and Petticoat, with a short working Apron over it, which discovered her shape to the most advantage. Her hair was cut up and divided very prettily, with several Ribbons stuck up and down in it. Her Head [commode] was extremely high. I was also offended by a small Patch she wore on her Breast, which I cannot suppose is placed there with any good Design. The Shop-Maid told me that Mademoiselle had something very curious in the tying of her Garters, but as I pay a due Respect even to a Pair of Sticks when they are under Petticoats, I did not examine into that Particular.

We learn from this that hoops had not yet reached France, where they did not become fashionable until after 1718; and that the commode was in fashion there after it had fallen in England. St Simon

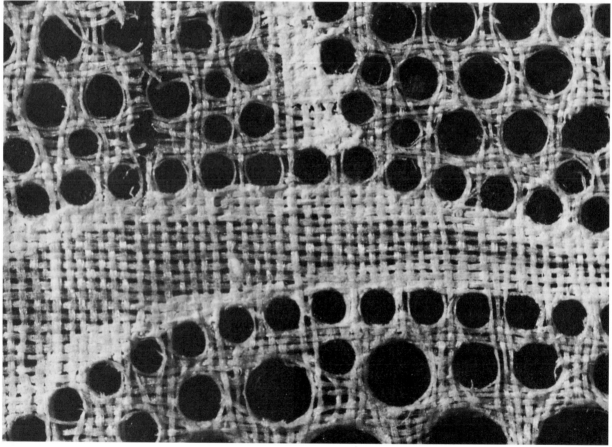

54 *(a) Pierced silk work, part of an apron border.*
   *(b) Detail, showing the use of different-sized bodkins
to produce a pattern of holes, each rimmed with gum to
keep it stiff.*

in his journal of the Court at Versailles relates in 1719 a story of a commode, though he makes it clear that it refers to an earlier time. As a lady at the supper table leaned forward to take salt for her boiled egg, her head was set on fire by the flame of a candle. Her quick-witted neighbour dashed it to the floor, but the lady, who had been unaware of the conflagration above her, and was now exposed as bald, rounded on him in a fury and threw her egg in his face so that it ran all over him. St Simon explains, 'She was wearing a coiffure called a commode which was not attached at all and which was put on and taken off just as men put on and take off a wig or a nightcap, and the mode was that these headdresses were very high.'

The raised headdresses, which had supported some of the most beautiful and finely textured laces the world has ever known, had thus disappeared in France before 1719. What remained was the semi-circular cap back, now placed flat on the top of the head with just a little frill at the front which might stand upright, or dip down in the centre of the forehead like a widow's peak (figs 52, 55); and the lappets, still formally obligatory for Court, but also worn casually in a variety of styles, a mode which was to remain popular almost continuously through much of the eighteenth and nineteenth centuries.

In 1713 the War of the Spanish Succession ended with the Spanish Netherlands ceded to Austria. In 1714 Queen Anne died. So, in 1715, did Louis XIV. It was a turning point in lace fashion. In general the English, following the bucolic habits of the Hano-verians, moved towards the relaxed comfort of country life, and as infrequently as possible towards the crowded and uncomfortable Birthdays and Drawing-rooms of Court with their inordinately complex regulations of dress. The French on the other hand, freed from the last dismal days of the Sun King, sped rapidly towards a Regency of licentious frivolity, under the guidance of Louis' nephew, the Duke of Orléans.

For men, lace worn with a three-piece suit made up of coat (frock), waistcoat (vest) and knee breeches, appeared only in three areas: at the neck as a cravat, at the wrists as simple ruffles attached to the shirt sleeves, and as a frilling on the front opening of the shirt which was allowed to emerge through the unbuttoned upper part of the vest as a chitterling (colour plate 3). This was a fashion which continued almost unchanged to the end of the century. The use of gold lace on coats and tricorne hats was discontinued after the 1750s, and cravats by that time were of plain linen, ritualistic-ally knotted but without lace.

For women, in the first half century, lace was

55 *A maid offers lace to her mistress. Note the difference in quality and quantity of lace between them.*

worn on the head as flat caps of varying styles such as the round-eared cap which curved down at the sides of the head, resting above the ears. The neckline of the chemise, or shift, visible above the low-cut bodice, carried an upright tucker of lace. The chemise sleeves, ending just below the elbow, supported a single ruffle. A handkerchief, folded into a triangle, hung over the bosom like a tippet, or might be looped round the neck like a cravat (fig. 60a).

These positions, and shapes, of lace differed little through the various styles of dress in those first 50 years. The type of lace, however, was adapted to their degree of formality or informality. The casual morning gowns, also known, as in the seventeenth century, as negligées, undress, nightgowns or des-habille, were often painted or printed cottons, and their accessories were of translucent muslin or lawn, gently gathered, sometimes plain, sometimes with chain-stitch embroidery of minute size, some-times with the most exquisitely detailed drawnwork incorporating an unbelievable variety of stitches (fig. 53). The finest qualities were associated with Saxony, and were known as Dresden work, but similar embroidered laces were made in Denmark.

Such laces also decorated the so-called close-

bodied or tight-bodiced gowns, a typically English fashion of the 1740s to '60s, beloved of the *nouveaux riches* as they were painted before their country mansions on their newly acquired estates. So fine was the muslin fabric which made the laces that it appears almost invisible in the portraits of Devis and others, no more than a whisper of mist to indicate a long apron, a tippet or a drooping cuff.

Laces were imitated in the mid-century by the piercing of pale ivory silks with bodkins or stilettos to make a pattern of holes of varying sizes. This created an openwork ground around solid areas, emphasized by white paint, which formed the design (fig. 54).

The decoration of more formal gowns (fig. 55) – the Court mantua and the sacque which was mainly French, demanded a more recherché lace, such as those of Flanders or France. On the sacque the close-fitting sleeves ended at the elbow with layered shells of fabric and, beneath these, stiff tiers of lace hung suspended, falling deeply below the elbow and shallowly above, in a style which persisted for some 50 years, between 1725 and 1775. Borders of lace or fabric, known as robings, passed down either side of the stomacher in a converging V, then separated to continue downwards clinging to the edge of the open skirt or, if the skirt was not open, then presenting the illusion that it was. On the head, a small flat cap with frills and lappets was often covered with a tippet of black silk worn like a mantilla.

In the Court mantua the open skirt of the dress was drawn back and looped up to expose a broad petticoat stretched over laterally distended hoops. The tall fontange which accompanied it during the first decade was, after that, replaced by a flat cap and

56 *Louis XIV, a wax profile by Antoine Benoist, 1715. There is Binche bobbin lace around the neck of his shirt.*

57 *The exquisite bobbin laces of Flanders, c.1675–1725.*

(a) Binche with snowball ground; (b) Mechlin showing the silky gimp and traditional ground; (c)

Valenciennes with an early five-hole ground; (d) Non-continuous Brussels, sometimes called point d'Angleterre.

(a)

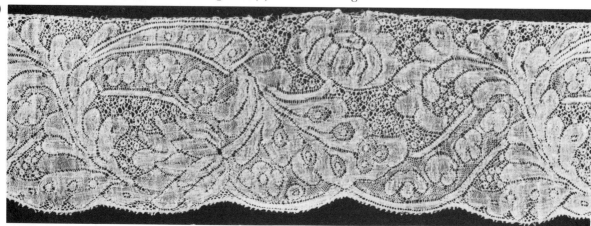

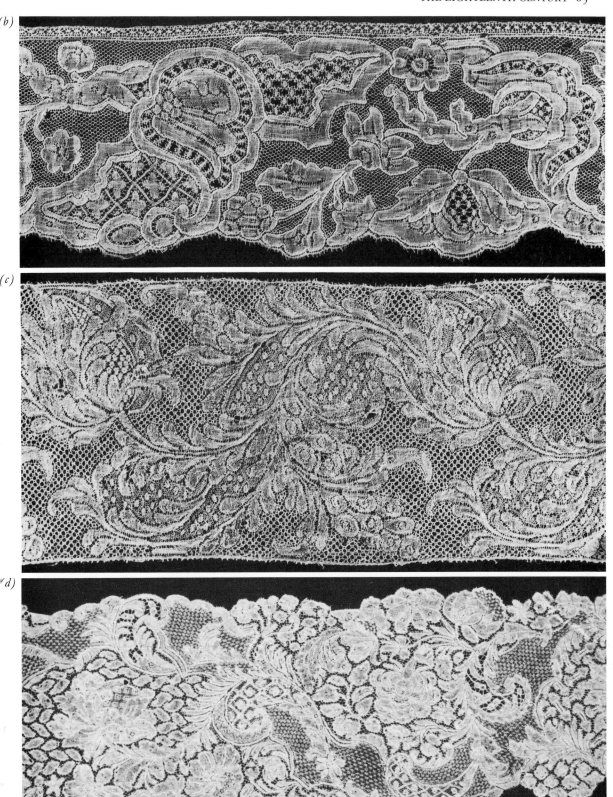

(b)

(c)

(d)

58 *(a) Robert Walpole, first Earl of Orford, Prime Minister 1721–42, by Van Loo c.1740. His cravat is of closely textured point d' Angleterre, probably of an earlier date.*

(b) A rare fan of point d' Angleterre lace, partly à brides *(with a guipure ground), partly* à reseau *(with a meshed ground). The sophisticated design is of a cherub playing beneath a fountain in a balustraded garden thick with flowers. c.1730.*

silver lace vied with ribbons, jewels, embroideries or brocaded silks to achieve an effect of the utmost richness (fig. 135).

Flanders, under a relatively stable Austrian sovereignty, had to some extent recovered its economic aplomb by 1715. The gossamer texture of its bobbin laces, made with a diaphanous flax thread of 1200 count, had now acquired distinctive features in different areas, such as Binche with its snowball ground, shown in a disseminated form in the wax portrait of Louis XIV (fig. 56). Though all these laces had in common the lovely naïve designs of plumply rounded flowers curving from leafy sprays, the ground, the outline, and the mode of construction could still distinguish them. In Binche laces the chubby fronds lay frozen in a curtain of snowflakes; in Mechlin a silky gimp bound the outlines of stalked blooms; in Valenciennes – a town by that time politically in France – an early five-hole ground became a roundly-plaited mesh, and then a square one, holding the buoyant pattern against a trellis of filigree; while Brussels laces, made non-continuously, raised a small three-dimensional rim around petals and leaflets, and linked their separate parts with the laboriously made droschel (figs 57, 58).

The emotive beauty of these laces was soon modified not only by the after-effects of many years of war, but also by the colder precision of a rationalistic age, and by the increasing stresses of a changing society which inhibited their childlike directness of expression. The lightweight designs, like an ethereal baroque, became as the years passed, a delicately cluttered rococo, and then the sprays of

hanging lappets of the finest quality lace. The neck might carry a lace cravat, or a collarette in the form of a little ruff; the chest a lace tucker, tippet and robings; the upper arms rows of tightly pleated ruffles with, in addition, two or three rows of engageants cascading from the sleeves of the hidden chemise, while on the petticoat bands of gold and

flowers became harder, less warmly spontaneous, entwined and imprisoned by formal garlands, and finally reduced in stature as the openwork part of the lace gained in importance, until by the end of the century only the ground remained, forming a plain net, unrelieved by any design.

In spite of all the import restrictions against them, which in France were particularly severe, the demand for Flemish laces remained so overwhelming that the needle laces of France were forced to copy them. As a result, the minute symmetrical detail of the original point de France was transformed in the second decade into two much lighter-weight laces which were named, after their centres in Normandy, Argentan and Alençon. Both now had the parts of their design linked not by bars but by a uniform mesh or reseau ground. Argentan appears over and over again with remarkable clarity in portraits, in the form of caps, ruffles, tuckers, cravats and tippets, and is shown with especial beauty in the portrait of Madame de Pompadour by Drouais (figs 59, 60).

The eighteenth century was a period of almost continual enmity between France and Britain so that for Britain it was the French laces which were most particularly excluded: in fact in 1745, following the second Jacobite rebellion, the Anti-Gallican Society vowed never again to wear French lace. Thus while French portraits tend to display their prestigious needle laces, English portraits more commonly depict bobbin laces or Dresden-style embroideries.

Even after their early recovery, the path of eighteenth-century laces was scarcely smooth. Their slender forms, instead of dominating the fashion scene, were becoming transformed into little more than foils for the magnificent brocaded silks now issuing from Spitalfields and Lyons, and though laces maintained their integrity into the mid-century, by the second half the designs of the lightly-textured monochromes, and even the perfection of their techniques, were of diminished importance. Ultimately it would be borne in on the socialites that a woven gauze, plain or patterned, could achieve the same effect as lace at a fraction of the cost (fig. 61).

Blows to lace in fashion now seemed to come from all sides. Literati set out to debunk it, as had Addison and Steele with their suave satires. Defoe in the 1720s aimed his barbs at the uncleanliness which fashion could hide, or which indeed the expense of lace might make unavoidable. Gentlemen in Paris committed to wearing lace bought ruffles even when they had no shirts to put them on, since a vest and coat garnished with lace could acceptably conceal a nakedness beneath; or having

59 *Madame de Pompadour, c.1760. Her cap of Argentan lace is tied beneath her chin; robings and tucker border the square neckline of her gown, which appears to be of painted silk. By Drouais, detail.*

one shirt only they were forced to wear it 15 days on end, powdering the lace at frequent intervals to refresh its brightness.[2] Unfortunately such whitening-powders often depended on lead oxide or other heavy metal poisons for their effect which, quite apart from being detrimental to health, had a devastating effect on the lace, for when exposed to sulphurous fumes, as from a domestic coal fire or industrial smoke, it underwent an irreversible conversion to grey lead sulphide. Similar disasters threatened the complexion of ladies visiting Bath where, they were warned, contact of the medicinal waters – which contained sulphur – with their 'white paint' might turn their skins 'entirely yellow if not black'.[3]

Swift, in a series of scurrilous poems in the 1720s and 30s, bit more deeply down to the obsessions which accompanied strict conformity to fashion: 'Five hours (and who can do it less in?), By haughty Celia spent in Dressing, The Goddess from her Chamber issues, Array'd in Lace, Brocade and Tissues.' Celia was not only vain, but unclean. Her cap and lappets were 'greasy Coifs and Pinners reeking, Which Celia slept at least a week in,' as she

60 *(a) The second wife of Chardin, hand-spinning with her elegant boudoir wheel, wears a stylish cap, cravat and engageants of superb Argentan, matching the cascades of lace which fill the bodice opening. The needle lace engageants are lengthened by a bobbin torchon lace sometimes called crâppone, so lightening the effect and reducing the cost. The petticoat flounces are of punched and ruched silk, matching the dress robings and jutting cuffs. Attributed to Francois Pouget, c.1770.*

(b) An Alençon jabot worn by the Rt Hon. John Hely Hutchinson, Secretary of State for Ireland, 1777–94. This is an example of anachronistic official wear: lace at the neck was out of fashion for everyday. By Sir Joshua Reynolds, c.1779.

may well have done, to avoid setting her coiffure afresh every day. Other evidence supports the adverse effect of fashion upon cleanliness, at this time, but the contrast between the external illusion of beauty and the squalor of the underlying reality is nowhere more brutally revealed than in Swift's scathing verses on *A Beautiful Young Nymph going to Bed*, which mercilessly rips aside the veil of privacy and pretension:

> Then seated on a three-legged chair, Takes off her artificial Hair. Her eyebrows from a Mouse's Hyde, Stuck on with art on either side. Now dexterously her Plumpers Draws, That serve to fill her hollow jaws. Untwist a wire and from her Gums, A set of Teeth completely comes. Pulls out the rags contrived to prop Her flabby Dugs and down they drop. Proceding on, the lovely Goddess, Unlooses next her Steel Rib'd Bodice. . . .

In England such pointed attacks, added to the torpid attitude of the Court towards fashion, had a depressing effect on clothes and laces until, com-

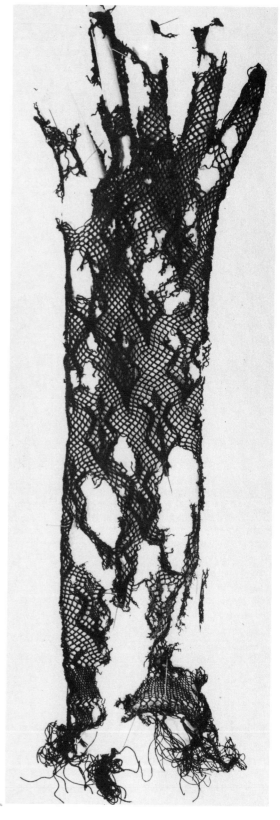

61 *(a) The substitution of gauze. A narrow silk lace lies along the top of the woven gauze which frills around the bodice and mob cap. The apron, spread over a round hoop, is of sprigged muslin. Hester Piozzi (Mrs Thrale), c.1785.*

(b) Mrs Thrale's black mittens may be made of sprang, like this pair from a Danish grave of the second half of the eighteenth century; or they may be of machine-made looped net.

bined with the dubious economic condition of the country as a whole, the highest quality of laces from abroad began to be replaced by more rapidly made, and therefore less expensive, imitations. There was also a renewed attempt to foster home production, in particular of the Devon (Honiton) laces. Swift's references to 'right Macklin' (Mechlin, or Malines), which was ardently sought and cost £12 a yard in 1729, indicates the existence of a spurious Mechlin, probably made in the East Midlands of England where the designs of the so-called Bucks point laces are sometimes deceptively similar to their Flemish counterpart. Even the distinctive Mechlin ground might be imitated, though Bucks workers were in general more at home with a Lille, or halfstitch, ground.

A similar process occurred in Denmark where the Tønder bobbin laces, produced by only seven lace-makers in 1717, occupied 10,000 workers by 1780, and the gross income from the sale of their lace had grown to 117,000 dalers (dollars, worth about 25p each). They sought to replace the sublime, but still

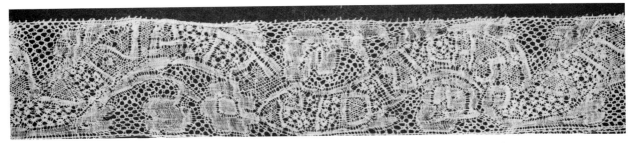

62 *Tønder bobbin lace, 1760, worked with the message VIVAT FRIDRICH 5 (reigned 1746–66). This commemorates the centenary of the constitutional revolution of 1660 when Frederick III conferred upon himself absolute monarchy.*

monstrously expensive, laces of Flanders, and to this end Flemish patterns were in one way or another copied, or stolen, and sometimes different grounds were used (fig. 62). A Tønder pattern book from the 1760s shows laces with that same bold and beautiful rotundity, in a *fond de neige* or snowball ground, which had graced the Binches and Valenciennes of several decades earlier.[4] In 1741 Tønder was so possessive of her developed skills that to avoid plagiarism traders had to swear under oath that they would not beguile any lace-maker to emigrate, just as had happened in Brussels in 1698, and in Britain under the Combination Acts for skilled workers in 1700. In addition, to prevent their escape, lace-makers needed passports to travel even from one duchy to another.[5]

Such developments pose a problem for the students of lace in fashion. Laces which look, in a portrait, as though they are clearly from a certain country and a certain time, may in fact be laces copied elsewhere and at a later date, so that the unwary may be beguiled into false conclusions.

Venice in the eighteenth century appears to have left few records of whatever survived of her commercial lace-making. But that she retained at least some ideas of her own we learn from Jean-Jacques Rousseau, who was Secretary to the French Ambassador there in 1743–4. In his *Confessions* he describes an encounter with a Venetian lady:

> I found her in an undress more than wanton, unknown to northern countries and which I will not amuse myself in describing though I recollect it perfectly well [more than 20 years later]. I shall only remark that her ruffles and collar were edged with silk network ornamented with rose-coloured pompoms. I found it to be the mode in Venice, and the effect is so charming that I am surprised it has never been introduced into France.[6]

1750s–1800

While the general trend of the quality of lace in fashion in the second half of the eighteenth century was in the direction of decadence, the powerful royal Courts continued to demand, and to get, the very best. The grotesque panier style of mantua, with the petticoat stretched seven feet wide over cane hoops, was at its broadest between 1740 and 1760 (see fig. 135). Only the protocol of death could diminish the splendour, and in Britain if death interfered with that grandest of occasions, the King's Birthday, then the corpse would have to wait. Horace Walpole records how Sophia (see fig. 47b) great granddaughter of Elizabeth of Bohemia

63 *(a) The Tsarina Elizabeth I, reigned 1741–62. Her magnificent Court dress is of rich brocade bejewelled with diamonds. The starched ruffles of lace which encrust her upper arms and edge her bodice are Russian in design.*

63 *(b) The Empress Maria Theresa, with matching cravat, tucker and ruffles. By M. Meytens, 1759.*

and sister of the reigning monarch George II, died most inconveniently on 11 November 1754, on the very eve of such a Birthday, when all the preparations were already completed. 'As *excessive* as the concern for her is at court,' he says, 'the whole royal family, out of great consideration for the mercers, lacemen etc., agreed not to shed a tear for her till tomorrow morning, when the birthday will be over; but then they will all rise by six o'clock to cry quarts.'[7]

In Russia, where belief in the divine right of kings persisted into the twentieth century, a portrait of the Tsarina Elizabeth I (see fig. 63(a)) shows her wearing the traditional pleated lace ruffles on the upper arm, and a lace tucker above a silver gown

encrusted with diamonds. The laces are marked with those sinuous trails so characteristic of Russian designs. Russia, like Denmark and Britain, had an extensive home industry at this time, and there is evidence of lace made in Minsk using thorns from the 'wild pear tree' as pins.[8] Bloated with dropsy and over-indulgence in French pâtés, the Tsarina took always a keen interest in French fashions, and died in 1761 leaving some 15,000 gowns of inordinate richness.

In 1761 Princess Charlotte of Mecklenburg-Strelitz married George III of Great Britain. Her wedding flounce, which is still in existence, was of Argentan lace, seven yards long and 27 inches wide. 'Her tiara of diamonds was very pretty,' wrote Walpole of the wedding, 'her stomacher sumptuous; her violet-velvet mantle and ermine so heavy that the spectators knew as much of her upper half as the King himself.'[9]

A Lady in the Dress of the Year 1761.

64 *The dress of the year, 1761.* The Ladies' Pocket Book, *1762.*

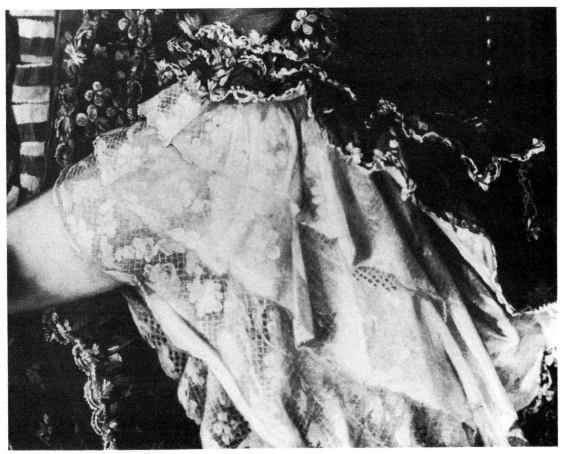

65 *Triple-tier blonde engageants. Detail from a*
'Portrait of a Lady', by Vestier, c.1760.

A superb portrait of the mid-eighteenth century, by Martin van Meytens (1695–1770) shows Maria Theresa, Queen of Hungary and Bohemia and Archduchess of Austria standing beside her triple crowns. Her magnificent mantua of pink silk is entirely covered with a gorgeous lace in which leafy palm trees soar over curling fronds, and meandering garlands enclose exotic fruits, hovering dragonflies and galaxies of stars. The accompanying stomacher, ruffles, robings, tippet and cravat appear to be all of matching lace. The august figure of the Empress, who reigned from 1740 to 1780, is mature and matronly, and she appears somewhat older than the 27 or 28 years which a postulated date of 1745 would make her. Indeed the remarkable similarity of feature, stance and tiara between this portrait and a second, also by van Meytens – in the Akademie der Bildenden Künste, Vienna – and dated 1759, suggests that the pink gown was part of the extravagant celebrations for the betrothal and marriage in 1760 of the Empress's eldest son, the future Emperor Joseph II (fig. 63(b)).

As for the lace itself, its chinoiserie nuance is reminiscent of mid-eighteenth century flounces of the French needle lace, Argentan. But France and Austria were enemies during the War of the Austrian Succession (1741–8), and in 1744–5 Louis XV conquered the Austrian Netherlands (Flanders) and went on to invade the United Provinces (now called Holland). In 1748 the Netherlands reverted to Austria, and for the next 35 years, until seized by France in 1794, Flanders enjoyed a period of almost unprecedented peace.

During the Seven Years War of 1756–63, France and Austria were allies. At the time Flanders prospered under the benign rule of Maria Theresa's brother-in-law, Charles of Lorraine, so that another possible source of the lace is Flanders. Actual records of lace worked in Flanders for the Empress, and incorporating the bobbin-made droschel, were researched by Paulis.[10] They relate to 'un habillement et une garniture' (an ensemble and a trimming) – though *ofte* (or) is used instead of *ende* (and) elsewhere in the Flemish of the original procès-

66 *The round gown of the 1780s, long-sleeved, low-necked and high-waisted, with the full skirt padded out at the back and sides. The central lady carries a knotting shuttle, of the type used in the nineteenth century for tatted lace; while the lady on the right works at a tambour frame, holding the thread above the fabric with her left hand. All three have bouffant fichus of muslin, or net. By Tomkins after Bunbury, 1789.*

verbal. This lace was apparently made in 1743, and the quoted value of 25,000 guldens, or Austrian florins, equivalent to over £3,000 at that time, suggests it was no mean specimen.

Such royal representatives of Russia, Great Britain and the Habsburg Empire related to an old order, the *ancien régime*, which was well on the way to passing. In contrast to them, the increasing numbers of *nouveaux riches*, buying or marrying their way into an upper middle-class society, launched their own fashion with simple bobbin laces which

had an effect of pretty prettiness rather than of exclusive grandeur.

Coincidentally with this development came books which gave not only information on what was being worn, but also advice. *The Ladies' Pocket Book* was first issued in 1759. 'The Manner of Dressing in the Year 1761' was described retrospectively by 'A Lady of Fashion':

For the head, fly and chevaux de frize lappets, the fly edged, and to be set with French beads [jet], or garnets. The hair frenched, the dress still more full if the lappets hang down [wider hoops for Court wear, when the lappets were not allowed to be pinned up]. For earrings, clusters; no drops unless in full dress with a hoop. For the neck, a large quantity of beads with a tippet hung careless; or, an esclavage [a series of gold chains] with a skin made of Italian gauze. The ruffles must be tripple, very full and deep, and by being trimmed with ribband they become still more fashionable. The negligée must be full, trimmed with blond and ribbon, and the train very long' (fig. 64).

1 Mary Bromley, daughter of Sir William Lygon, aged 18. Circle of Robert Peake, 1623. There is an interesting harmony between the bobbin lace which encircles the bodice, and the needle lace on the standing collar which frames her head.

2 The Emperor Leopold I of Austria, Holy Roman Emperor, reigned 1657-1705. By Jan Thomas, *c*.1660. He is in theatrical dress, as a shepherd, in the current fashion of short-sleeved doublet and loose-ended breeches, with plenty of gold lace to indicate his divine origin.

Novices are advised not to follow extremes of fashion too closely, for they may be unbecoming:

> I have seen some few nights ago at the boxes [theatre], some ladies who intended to be particularly fine, by having their heads dressed en tête de mouton [literally sheep's head, that is with the hair piled high and powdered white], because the ladies in Paris dress in that manner; and what was the consequence? the ladies looked like so many ghosts. That manner of dressing the head is ridiculous, unless the cheeks are painted the depest shade of vermilion; thus tho' it might be becoming in Paris, where they paint high, yet it was intolerable here.

Lady Mary Wortley Montagu's comment was more pithy: 'Their woolly hair and fiery faces make them look more like skinned sheep than human beings.'[11]

The 'blond' mentioned in the *Pocket Book* as trimming the morning gown or negligée was a French bobbin lace made of silk thread of two different thicknesses which gave it the appearance of glistening blobs of pale gold set in a spider's web of almost invisible fineness. It was used for engageants (fig. 65), tuckers and tippets, as the earlier Flemish laces had been, and it severely affected their production. A traveller to Mechelen in 1755 observed that the convents were thinking of 'giving up the trade as the English, upon whom they depended, have taken to the wearing of French blondes.'[12] Blondes remained popular until the French Revolution (1789–93), with the subsequent Napoleonic Wars, severely interrupted cross-Channel trade.

Other French bobbin laces became equally popular, such as the Chantilly made of matt silk instead of a glossy one, and often dyed black; and Lille and point de Paris laces, both made with linen thread.

England, under the encouragement of George III, had itself shown some signs of becoming, in a modest way, self-sufficient in lace. The influx of French blondes disrupted this progress, and a petition from the lace-makers of Olney, in Bedfordshire, in 1780, described them as starving. The cessation of importations from France, at the time of the Revolution, inspired the East Midlands to fill the gap by copying Lille designs, and also the point de Paris ground which was known locally as wire ground or Kat stitch. Even silk blondes and Chantillys were imitated, though with simplified designs.

All these bobbin laces, so infinitely simpler, so vulgarly more obvious, than the beautiful Flemish laces of the first half of the century, were encouraged by a social process of democratization, as well as by a simplification of dress style which began in the 1760s. The 'round gown', keeping the low-cut bodice of the sacque and of the close-bodied gowns, had the décolletage filled in with a bouffant tippet or fichu, which was usually of muslin or gauze rather than lace. The fitting sleeves extended to the wrists, and had small frilly ruffles. The flat little cap and lappets swelled upwards into a balloon-like mob cap trimmed with ribbons, and a thin border of blonde. The skirt, cut a little shorter than the older styles, exposed the ankles, and it was at this point that hand-knitted stockings and mittens, imported from Spain and decorated with openwork, started a trend which was to lead to the very first machine laces (see figs 66, 140b).

These were made on the knitting machine, or Stocking Frame, originally invented in the sixteenth century, but having no connection with lace until the eventful 1760s. By that time the faultless Flemish laces, still using their exquisitely fine flax thread, were being forced by economic conditions into plainness. The delicate meshes of droschel, scrupulously arranged in thin ranks, were aligned into veils so fine that one square yard weighed a fraction of an ounce, and so immaculate that they were priced, c.1800, at £60.

It was this kind and quality of flawless mesh which the dexterous machine workers (framework-knitters) aimed to copy. From that time on, veils of translucent lawn, filmy muslins or silk gauze, were gradually replaced by veils of plain or patterned net, in effect by lace.

The first machine nets, since they were made on the Stocking Frame, were knitted ones, but within a decade they had become so fine that the tiny looped stitches which made them could scarcely be seen with the naked eye. In a short time the regularity of the mesh was so perfect that apart from the difference in materials, linen thread for droschel and silk for the Stocking Frame; and a subtle difference in colour – the droschel white marginally tinged with grey, the knitted production (known as point net, or tulle) having the palest glint of gold – they could well be mistaken for each other.

These point nets, also known as patent nets, were immensely popular (fig. 67). Though the process was invented in England, Louis XVI in 1774 arranged for one of the machines to be pirated, so that the production of patent nets in France did not lag far behind.

It became fashionable to wear these veils of net in the shape of long stoles or broad scarves, drooped forward over the face and falling on either side almost to the floor. The head itself tended to droop, and the body leaned forward a little from the hips as

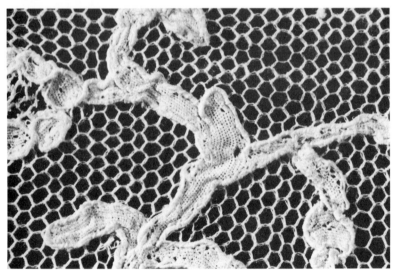

67 *(a) A cap of looped net. The crown can be tightened around the head by a draw-string, while the short veil falls forward over the face.*

(b) Detail of the machine-knitted net and the motifs of Alençon applied to it.

if the wearer were caught up in the agonies of a Greek tragedy. As the trend strengthened during the 1770s, veils 'à l'Iphigenie' followed the first performance in Paris of Gluck's *Iphigenie en Aulide* in 1774, and *Iphigenie en Tauride* in 1779.

The round gowns, by the 1780s, were being supplemented by simpler gowns of white cotton sometimes known as chemise gowns, or Creole-style, a fashion said to have been started by Marie Antoinette (1755–93). The loose form of the dress, and the name, both derived from the Creoles of Louisiana, USA, French-speaking descendants of French emigrés who had settled there in the time of Louis XIV.

The chemise dress had a negative effect on lace in fashion, the lack of contrast depriving it of any noticeable effect.

By 1790 the cotton gowns were attenuating into sheaths of drapery, straight and high-waisted (fig. 68), with contrasting tunics of black or coloured knotted net draped over them, or stoles, veils and shawls variously entwined around them. The nets were sometimes decorated with running or chain-stitch embroidery (see fig. 76), or with the application of decorative sprigs made by a bobbin or needle lace technique. Narrow little laces of Lille, Bucks, Mechlin or blonde, inconspicuously patterned, were sparingly used to trim the neckline or sleeve ends. The mob caps of inflated muslin had gone, and by the end of the century close-fitting caps made of bobbin lace, sprigged muslin or embroidered net covered the shortened hair, and fastened neatly beneath the chin. So plain and slim did the dresses become that one might imagine Mrs Delany's prediction of 1747 to have come true:

> They curl and wear a great many *tawdry* things. . . . The only thing that seems general are hoops of an enormous size, and most people wear vast winkers on their heads. They are now come to such an extravagance that I expect soon to see the other extreme, and from appearing like so many *blown bladders* we shall look like so many *bodkins stalking about*.[13]

It was not a profitable time for hand-made laces. They were a commodity made for trade, and they would survive commercially as long, but only as long, as there was a demand which they could supply. Even in the royal Courts elaborate laces emerged only for special functions, and monarchy itself was an endangered species. In the wealthy middle classes however fashion retained its powerful hold, and Napoleon Bonaparte, the machines, and human vanity were, between them, soon to revive lace in fashion.

68 *The neo-classical style, antipathetic to lace. The contrast of the simplicity of these plain draperies with all the gaudy excesses of previous decades could hardly be more extreme. 'The Archers', by Wright and Zeigler, after Adam Buck, 1799.*

4
The Nineteenth Century
FROM COURT TO SALON

1800–1820

The stark and laceless simplicity of line which had characterized the end of the eighteenth century was carried over into the early nineteenth. The dresses of muslin were cut so low that their necklines almost met the high waistlines, exposing wide areas of bare skin beneath a naked throat (fig. 69). The fine cotton clung to women's figures so that they must have appeared like those wayward goddesses of ancient Greece and Rome whose warm flesh glows through aery swirls in the paintings of Raphael and Titian.

But not everyone was young and shapely, nor was it always summer, and no doubt in spite of thick body stockings worn underneath and warm Kashmir shawls wrapped above, many of the ladies died of pneumonia. Between cold, discomfort and moral disapproval it was not long before elaboration in dress appeared, a process which was assisted by the unlikely person of Napoleon Bonaparte.

(a)

Napoleon had risen by the end of 1799 to the position of First Consul of France, and he was crowned Emperor in 1804. His intention was to re-establish the glory of France which he felt to have been degraded by a decadent Bourbon monarchy. He revived the French laces, wrecked by the Revolution, and adopted the needle lace Alençon for official Court wear, which it had been in the time of Louis XVI and Marie Antoinette, guillotined only 11 years before. At his coronation Napoleon wore a small ruff and cravat of Alençon, while his wife Josephine, resplendent in ivory satin, wore a standing collar of the same lace above a deep décolletage.

The making of the silk blonde and Chantilly laces, which had been popular in the second half of the eighteenth century, was also revived, as well as Flemish bobbin laces, for Flanders, freed at long last from Habsburg domination, was now securely in the hands of the French, along with Holland, Switzerland, Venice, Milan and parts of central Italy. Napoleon was partial to Mechlin, to which lace he poetically compared the spires of Antwerp Cathedral; but his favourite was that type of Brussels bobbin lace of rich design embedded in a droschel ground, and formerly marketed under the name point d'Angleterre.

At Napoleon's second wedding, in 1810, to Marie Louise of Austria, daughter of the Emperor Franz, and granddaughter of Marie Antoinette's brother Leopold II, the bride's wedding veil was of Brussels bobbin appliqué, bearing the initial M beneath the Napoleonic eagle and the Imperial crown, while the light ground, made of thread finer than gossamer, was diapered with bees, symbolic of Bonaparte (fig. 70).

In the interest of promoting Lyons silks,

69 *(a) Neo-classical dress of the turn of the century. Compare classical dress, fig. 2a. The low-cut neckline bears the thinnest sliver of lace, the net sleeves are embroidered with tambour work. 'Young Lady', by Robert Lefebvre, 1805.*

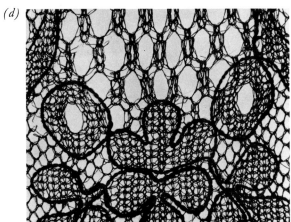

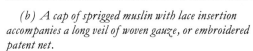

*(b) A cap of sprigged muslin with lace insertion
accompanies a long veil of woven gauze, or embroidered
patent net.*

*(c) A bonnet veil of coffee-coloured silk gauze, woven
with curled fronds in an Indo-Spanish style. The regular
repeat indicates the use of the Jacquard. After 1803.*

(d) Detail of a patterned warp lace.

*(e) A tunic of embroidered patent net shields a dress
of muslin. Designed for the Sea Coast Promenade, 1809.*

70 *The wedding veil of Marie Louise. The fine droschel ground is made of narrow strips invisibly joined. The bobbin design, including the martial ranks of bees, is hand-stitched to the droschel. Brussels, 1810.*

Napoleon suppressed the importation of muslin. In England, currently at enmity with France, muslin continued to be worn, for while homegrown silk was of vital importance to the economy of France, cotton had become of vital importance to England.

The popularity of cotton had been on the increase ever since the founding of the East India Company in 1600, followed by the acquisition of the formerly Portuguese possession of Bombay in 1660. French possessions in India were acquired in 1763 at the end of the Seven Years War; and the first shipments of cotton wool from British colonies in the southern states of North America arrived in 1775.

However, the use of cotton for lace had always been restricted by the difficulty of obtaining a suitable thread. That from India was too fine, while English spinners, accustomed to the long, smooth suppleness of flax, seemed unable to adapt to the twisting of the shorter, more resilient fibres of the imported cotton. They had, perhaps, no great incentive, for England by the second half of the eighteenth century was well on the way to becoming an industrial country.

The successful mechanization of cotton spinning was begun by Hargreaves in 1766. His Spinning Jenny produced a thread adequate for weaving but too bumpy either for hand-made laces, where it

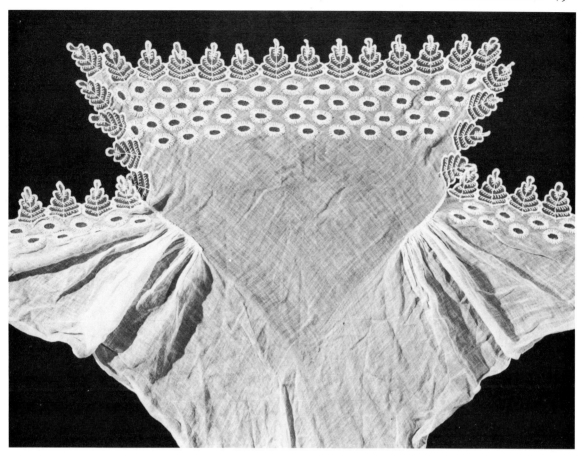

71 *A muslin chemisette, gathered over the shoulders, and with a standing collar. The embroidered leaves and flowers are centred with bobbinet, showing that it dates from after Heathcoat's invention of 1808.*

hampered the repeated pulling of the threads together to make an even tension, or for the Stocking Frame, where the irregularities caught in the beards of the needles.

The nets produced by the Stocking Frames were thus restricted to silk almost to the end of the eighteenth century. By that time a frame, of a type known as the Pin machine, had been smuggled into France and was pouring out silk 'point net' to such an extent that in the early nineteenth century it was in danger of flooding the English market.

Improvements in mechanical cotton spinning by Arkwright and Crompton in the 1770s soon enabled looped nets of cotton to be made on the Warp Frame. Yet another English machine was able to use cotton right from the start. This was the first machine to be invented specifically for the manufacture of fashion nets. It was called the Bobbin Net

machine, and was patented by John Heathcoat in 1808. It worked on a principle of twisting the threads rather than looping them, and copied the techniques of bobbin lace-making rather than those of knitting. Heathcoat indeed owed his original inspiration to watching a Bucks point lace-maker at work.

Modified in 1809 and named the Old Loughborough, his Bobbinet machine, through its use of preferentially imported cotton, had the advantage of reduced costs and thus of an availability to a much wider area of the public. The net-making machines could not use linen thread, for their jarring tensions would shatter the fragile fibres. Hand-made laces on the other hand had no really satisfactory cotton available until 1835 when Robert's Self-acting Mule was perfected.

There was thus in these first two decades of the nineteenth century a dichotomy into silk and cotton machine nets, and linen laces made by hand and frequently very plain. Only a mere pittance of a wage for the hand lace-workers could keep production viable for the traders, while skilled machine-workers (called framework-knitters and twist

72 *The marriage of the Princess Charlotte of Wales to Leopold, later first King of the Belgians, in 1816. Her wedding dress is of warp net studded with silver, her train of cloth of silver.*

73 *Princess Charlotte by G. Dawe, 1817. Loose sleeves of French blonde, the edges caught together with jewelled clasps, emerge from beneath her rich blue tunic.*

hands) faced with an expanding market, could soon demand almost 20 times as much.

Two other immensely important English machines, subsequently known as the Pusher and Leavers, date from this period. Beginning in 1812 and 1813 respectively they were at first, like the Old Loughborough, and the Stocking and Warp Frames, only two or three feet wide, and were worked at home, but within a few decades they had become enormous, involving tens of thousands of threads, and needing factories to house them.

These early machines gave England a tremendous advantage over France which as a mainly agricultural country did very little machine inventing. However, in spite of a prohibition on the export of textile machines, in force between 1782 and 1843, an Old Loughborough slipped through the fingers of the Customs men, just as the Pin machine had in 1774, and arrived in France in 1815. It was set up near Calais and commissioned to make an entire dress of net for the Duchess of Angoulême,[1] formerly the Princess Royal (Madame Royale), daughter of Marie Antoinette. Thus the seal of royal approval was given to machine laces.

In England, in the following year, 1816, a knitted

net made on a Warp Frame machine was used for the wedding dress of Princess Charlotte, daughter of the Prince Regent. It was of off-white silk, spotted with a silver tinsel which sparkled over it like miniature confetti (fig. 72).

The smuggling of the Old Loughborough into France had taken place during Napoleon's last Hundred Days. With the ending of hostilities, and the reinstatement of the Bourbon monarchy in the person of Louis XVIII, brother of the guillotined Louis XVI, silk hand-made laces from France deluged the English market, ending the dominance of those pale laces of linen which had embellished the misty clouds of muslin in neo-classical days. In 1817 a painting of the Princess Charlotte showed her wearing a royal blue gown from which emerged sleeves of warmly glowing 'Spanish blonde' (fig. 73).

Chantillys and Alençons, even if still only sparsely patterned, were a welcome change; while the silk looped nets, along with the cotton twist nets, gave employment at first to hundreds, later to thousands, of women and children in the Nottingham area, busily decorating veils, stoles, caps, fichus and pelerines with hand embroidery.

1820–1840

The early 1820s became a period of unparalleled prosperity. Fortunes from the various machines were made overnight. Middle-class manufacturers, suddenly elevated into prolific wealth, knew neither how to dress nor how to behave in the society to which they now sought admission. The subsequent attitudes of aggression and imitation were perhaps predictable. Suspicious of originality, and wary of creativeness, the ego-sensitive arrivistes sought safety in copying the Elizabethan, the gothic, and the Stuart styles. In time, Watteaus, Pompadours, polonaises and many others crowded the fashion scene in a regressive welter of throwbacks mingled in confusion.

It was at such ladies that the fashion journals aimed their seductive engravings. Where the seventeenth century had recorded the dress of men and women at the royal court (as in Bonnart's *Costume du Regne de Louis XIV*), and the eighteenth-century *Pocket Books* the prescribed dress of Hanoverian Drawing-rooms, the new fashion plates – from *Le Journal des Dames et des Modes* (1797–1839), *La Belle Assemblé* (1806–68), Ackermann's *Repository of the Arts* (1809–28), Godey's *Ladies' Book* (1830–98), and others – aimed lower and hit harder.

The frequent compulsive changes required by fashion soon became almost frenetic, with different dresses obligatory for the public promenade, the morning visit, the carriage, the seaside, the evening, the opera, the dinner, the ball. And laces, hand or machine, were needed to assist the variety. But these were for women only. The newly rich businessmen had, even more than their wives, to play for safety since they could neither offend their friends nor delight their rivals by appearing at any time incorrectly attired. Men's suits, as the decades passed, became ever more self-effacing and anonymous, proclaiming them not as individuals but as members of a type. Their clothes were not so much a decoration as a badge of office, any deviations from which might render a man *déclassé*. In this new and dowdy sobriety, lace and masculinity were no longer compatible. Indeed, lace for men assorted ill with increasing industrialization, the quickening tempo of life, and the gradual erosion of noble indolence.

Such an attitude may have been reinforced by the unpopularity of the Prince Regent, later George IV, and his associated Dandies. A verse of this time, called *The Political House that Jack Built*, describes the condition of the people as 'all tattered and torn, On account of taxation too great to be borne', the fault of 'the Dandy who bows with a grace, And has taste in wigs, collars, cuirasses and lace.'[2] When George

74 *The formal Court dress of the reign of George III, worn by Princess Charlotte. The eighteenth-century hoop, blowing out the skirt, may help to hold in place the almost non-existent bodice. The shrubbery of lace encircling her neck, and edging the sleeves and train, is lightweight and of slight design. c.1814.*

died in 1830 it was proposed by a Mr James M.P. that the coronation of William IV be done away with *in toto* as a useless ceremony. Failing in this, he proposed that its total cost be reduced from £50,000 to £5,000.[3]

Lace in fashion for men was thus finally out, except at Court where traditional, almost static, modes persisted in lace cravats and ruffles, worn with eighteenth-century-style coats and knee-length breeches. The coronation gear of Charles X, crowned King of France in 1824, harked as far back as trunk hose, ribbon gallants, and a riot of silver lace and tissue, as in portraits of Louis XIV in State dress in the mid-seventeenth century. For women, those great barrel-like hoops, out of fashion for decades in the social world, were obligatory for Court wear until the 1830s (fig. 74). Lappets, graduated in length by the social status of the wearer, were replaced only slowly by the new style of net veil which was scarcely accepted, fully, until

75 *Queen Adelaide's coronation dress, 1830. The Honiton sprigs along the hem, and spread down her skirt* en tablier, *spell out the letters of her name. By John Simpson, 1830.*

the end of the century. Court wear now lacked that critical time limit which fashion demanded: its conception of 'for the time being' was for a very long time indeed.

So the rift between Court and fashion widened. The rich of the middle classes, grasping the reins of fashion in their eager hands, set about galloping wildfire through the prestigious costumes of the past.

Meanwhile the great influx of French laces had done the English lace-makers no good at all. So destitute were they that in 1830 they sent a petition to Queen Adelaide, then Duchess of Clarence, begging her to patronize their products. The famous dress which resulted was worn at her husband's coronation in that year. It consisted of sprigs of Honiton mounted on bobbinet made at Heathcoat's factory, which had moved to Tiverton in Devon in 1816. The sprigs took the form of flowers whose romantic-sounding names – Amaranth (love-lies-bleeding), Daphne (a kind of laurel or bay tree), Eglantine (wild rose), Lilac, Auricula (a primula), Ivy, Dahlia, and Eglantine again – spelt out the letters of ADELAIDE (fig. 75).

It seems likely that the Queen also patronized East Midlands laces, for a portrait of her by Sir William Beechey shows sleeves of blonde similar to those worn by the Princess Charlotte, but of a flimsier texture – and blonde was soon to go quite out of fashion.

By 1831 the market was flooded with machine laces, and a period of depression for that industry set in which was to last until machine-patterning on an extensive scale began. Queen Adelaide was again petitioned, this time by the machine manufacturers, and now she ordered a dress of the finest possible bobbinet to wear at the Juvenile Ball held on 24 May 1831, in honour of the Princess Victoria of Kent, later Queen Victoria. The net was made of single, unplyed, strands of Italian silk, embroidered by hand in a design of circlets of roses in a floss silk so lustrous that it had 'more the appearance of mother of pearl than any other substance.'[4]

Almost to the end of these two decades the nets came off the machines plain, and the only way of decorating them was by hand embroidery. The run, or needlerun, technique began in Nottingham, and had spread by the 1830s to Limerick in Ireland. Tambour, or chain-stitch, embroidery on patent nets, which had been popular in France in the late eighteenth century, had become established in England, at Coggeshall, in the 1820s, but using bobbinet. Again the technique spread to Ireland where it became known as Limerick tambour (fig. 76).

Decoration by appliqué work, that is the attachment of bobbin or needle-made motifs to a net by means of a tedious knotted stitch made from the reverse side, dated back to the late eighteenth century. The wedding veil of Marie Louise in 1810, and the coronation gown of Queen Adelaide in 1830, were both of this type. The application of muslin, with the motifs delineated and held to the net by a couched cord, had begun in the 1820s, and

76 *A double pelerine collar, separated to show the two layers of tamboured net, with a thin edging of Bucks point, or similar lace, around the outside.* c.1830.

77 *'Newest Fashions' for February 1832. The little ruff, the exaggerated bodice and swollen sleeves, are all there, along with a bonnet veil which could be drawn forward over the face like a curtain. Said to be the Countess of Carmarthen in evening dress.*

the resulting fabric was known as Carrickmacross. An attempt to economize on the labour involved in this work was made by John Heathcoat in 1837 (patent no. 7359). It was 'for a mode of ornamenting gauze, muslin, or net, by adding figures to the surface by adhesion from using size, pressing the net and flowered work through rollers, and thus causing the superimposed ornaments to adhere.' This idea, though initially labour-saving, was not popularly adopted: when the nets were washed the glue dissolved and the detached motifs floated away and rose to the surface of the water.

The hand-embroidered nets were often much prettier than the contemporary bobbin laces. In addition they were cheaper, and could be made in larger pieces. They became so plentiful during the 1830s that prices fell. This was a disaster for the industry, and the original Limerick tambour bus-

iness died out in 1842; but it was a miracle for poorer people accustomed to regarding lace as a luxury for ever beyond their reach. As they picked up the falling crumbs of fashion, the market for lace became enlarged, while at the same time the once clearly defined barriers and exclusive perimeters of the fashionable world became obscured.

Apart from embroidered nets, the white embroidered muslins with their drawnworks and fine needle lace fillings to the hearts of flowers, remained popular long after the muslin gowns which they originally decorated had gone from fashion. Triangular fichus, single or double-tiered little capes known as pelerines, chemisettes with standing collars pierced with small windows filmed over again with net, still made charming accessories for dresses which during the 1830s were becoming far less simple.

Dresses swelled in the sleeves and skirt, and shrank in the bodice, presaging the age of the crinoline. The Regulations for Court Dress in 1834 required 'blonde lappets, a corsage trimming à la Medici, balloon-like upper sleeves à la Mameluke, and little ruffs à la Queen Elizabeth, the whole shrouded in a mantle of tulle illusion embroidered with gold' (see fig. 77). The quaint terms, appropriate for that fossilization of style which had become wedded indissolubly to the formality of the Court, was the clearest possible indication of the deepening rift between royalty itself and the bourgeois fashion scene where changes were frequent, precipitous and of sharp concern. Two or three decades later the climbing bourgeois themselves adopted such terms.

Queen Victoria, at her wedding in February 1840, followed Adelaide's example in patronizing English laces. The veil, flounce, collar and cuffs of her gown were of the quite newly-invented three-twist bobbinet with its light diamond-shaped meshes, as opposed to Heathcoat's original two-twist net with its round or softly hexagonal meshes. To this were attached large, bold and ornately imposing Honiton sprays made – as one might expect of the Court – 'in imitation of old'.[5] In the design, formal symmetry was linked with majestic flowers erupting from stems whose curled tips formed enclosures for sumptuous decorations (fig. 78). More than anything, the design recalls Jacobean crewel-work embroideries of the seventeenth century, in which the branching Tree of Life arises, Indian-style, from a base of low hills. The rich Eastern nuance which permeates it pays admirable tribute to Victoria, Queen of Great Britain, Empress of India.

With commendable diplomacy the Queen also bought Bucks point laces, some made at the school of Paulerspury in Northamptonshire, to embellish her trousseau.

The livelihood of East Midlands lace-makers nevertheless remained precarious. Stage coach travellers along the Great North Road were besieged at every stop by pedlars trying to sell them laces. Lace merchants' sample books of this period show the numbered pattern(s) which each lace-maker could work, so that when one had been chosen by the customer the order could be allocated to the appropriate maker, who all her life might make only one or two designs. This method achieved some semblance of specialization, with increased speed and efficiency of production. Some of the patterns could be made in black instead of white 'at an advance in the price of about 3d in every shilling'. This 25 per cent increase was to compensate for the difficulty of working with the dark thread which,

except in the most advantageous illumination, tended to lose itself in shadow.

Yet those who worked in the factories making machine laces were perhaps even worse off. Children were employed at cut-rate wages, and had to be intermittently thrashed to keep them awake. Not until 1833 was it made illegal to employ children under nine years of age, or to make nine to 13 year olds work more than 48 hours a week, or 13 to 18 year olds more than 69 hours. For adults the working day was unlimited until the Ten-hour Bill was finally passed in 1847.

The 1840s

A tremendous advance in mechanization marked the beginning of the fourth decade as a turning point for lace in fashion. The automatic patterning of machine laces, successful, after many attempts, at the end of the 1830s, enabled the Jacquard apparatus to implement a frothy torrent of shawls, flounces, mantelets, veils and insertions which were pouring out to every corner of a seemingly inexhaustible market. Patterning was particularly successful on the Leavers machine, which in France was referred to simply as 'the Jacquard'.

The success of these machine laces was partly determined by their low price, but mainly by an intense visual impact which made them easy to understand. The importance of this aspect was linked to the reliance of ladies on flat two-dimensional drawings for their knowledge of lace in fashion. Gone was that tactile sensibility which had come in the past from actual laces worn by the Fashion Dolls or Babies who travelled so hazardously across sea and land, enabling women both to feel the laces they wore and to examine them minutely. Deprived of this, all the nineteenth-century ladies could do was to look at the pictures. Thus what came to matter was not so much that the lace was right, as that it looked right. Machines were already masters of this sort of illusion.

It was the technique of hand-made meshes which had set the whole bobbinet industry in motion. Now, every scrap of bobbin lace that was found became the object of scrutiny as a potential pattern for machine copying, and this regardless of its age or place of origin – which would in fact seldom be known to the manufacturer. Soon, they were able to make copies so perfect – even including the imperfections present in the hand-made sample – that from a few feet away original and imitation could not be distinguished. It was to most ladies of fashion of minimal interest that as one approached more closely to hand-made laces, they increased in

beauty as the incisive clarity of their thread movements became more sharply defined, while machine laces approached closely showed a progressive diminution in attractiveness as their ugly distortions, tight pillaring and untidy angularities were revealed.

In such a philistine atmosphere, the exquisite subtlety of old Flemish laces, or the sweetly plain Bucks point, was the very last thing the members of new society wanted. Their wealth and position had to be obviously eye-catchingly displayed so that

78 *A corner of Queen Victoria's wedding veil. The effect of the antique design is heightened by leadwork fillings. Made of Honiton bobbin lace, worked at Beer, and attached to a machine-made diamond net. February 1840.*

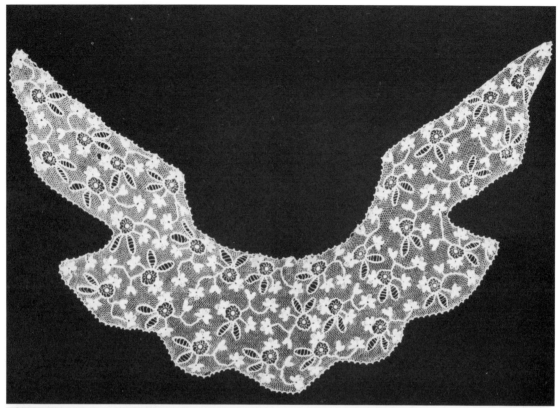

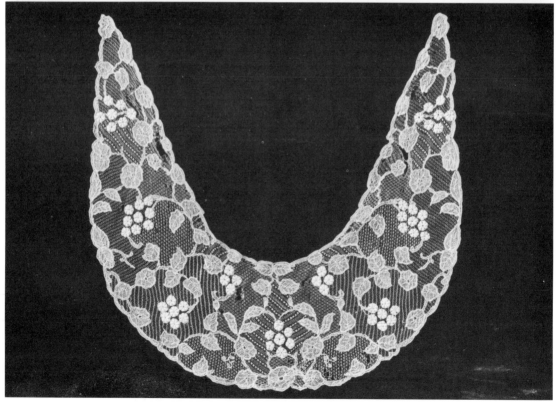

79 *(a) A collar of Irish crochet.*

(b) Carrickmacross or muslin appliqué, with varied decorative fillings of Limerick work (darned net). Both 1840s.

they could not possibly be overlooked. The swelling hoops of the crinolines were inflations of their egos, and skirts became ever more ostentatiously enlarged until ladies had to be warned: 'If she suffers much from the comments of vulgar little boys it would be better, in a high wind, to remain indoors.' Such vast expanses of cloth needed vastly obvious laces, and machines and craft between them were becoming set to satisfy that need.

The delicate white embroideries carried over from the 1830s survived for a little while on chemisettes bearing neat round collars of a type to be known in the twentieth-century as Peter Pan's. Undersleeves, extending from wrist to elbow, were known nostalgically and in the French mode as engageants. But the general style of dress had soon to discard them as insufficiently conspicuous.

The emergence of craft laces, scarcely in competition with the machines, but at a domestic level catering for the lower end of the fashion market, dates also from this decade. It was linked with distress caused by quite extraneous factors such as the potato famine in Ireland, which reduced the population of that country by some one and a half million people, or a sixth of its total. The magistrate of Cork, visiting the village of Skibbereen in 1846, reported:

> In the first hovel six famished and ghastly skeletons were huddled in a corner. I approached with horror and found that they were alive. In a few minutes I was surrounded with 200 such phantoms. Two dogs were shot while tearing a body to pieces. A starving cat was eating a dead infant.[6]

Attempts to develop and commercialize craft laces belong to these hungry '40s. Irish crochet and tatting, in addition to the Carrickmacross and other embroidered nets already established, were taught to the poverty-stricken families, mainly by nuns (fig. 79). But while the craft laces offered some hope of subsistence for the starving Irish, the bobbin lace-makers of England suffered from this additional competition.

Craft and other hand-made laces were often marketed through charitable agencies, but it was department stores in London and Paris which dealt with the machine laces, selling them in vast yardages, or as piece goods, over the counter. One of the first such stores was Swan and Edgar in Piccadilly. Here, in 1837, a 12-year old boy, Charles Frederick Worth, had begun his apprenticeship.

In France, in 1848, in yet another revolution, Louis Philippe d'Orléans was deposed, and power passed back again from Bourbon to Bonaparte, in the person of Napoleon III, son of Napoleon I's brother Louis, King of Holland, who had married Josephine's daughter by her first marriage, Hortense. Following a violent coup d'état in 1851, he was crowned Emperor in 1852, and the Second Empire began, some ten years after the onset of Victorian Britain.

The 1850s

Very importantly, the use of the Jacquard apparatus had opened the way for really large pieces of lace, most particularly flounces, veils which swept the ground, and long trains for Court or bridal wear. The best were still expensive, but there were plenty of lesser pieces geared to the lower end of the market.

Increasing literacy and, concurrently, a decreased tax on paper and newsprint in England meant that there was something to read for those who could. The soil was ready for the First International Exhibition, of 1851, organized by Prince Albert with the help of Henry Cole. Within seven months, a million square feet of glass supported by 2,300 steel girders, was set up over 19 acres in Hyde Park. It housed some 14,000 exhibition stands, lasted five months, and attracted over six million visitors.[7] By its lucrative prizes it stimulated British manufacture; by bringing in foreign goods it opened a kind of Pandora's box of new ideas which affected even lace with a mixed blessing.

The Exhibition brought back to fashion the idea of guipure laces. These were resurrections of seventeenth-century forms – before grounds of hand-made meshes (reseaux) had developed – when voluptuous designs were linked by short strands of thread, variously known as bars, brides, bridges or legs, which might be plaited, twisted or oversewn. Up to 1850 the lace of the English East Midlands was Bucks point. From the meshes, or halfstitch ground, of this lace, Heathcoat has taken the idea for his net, while the ease with which its simplistic designs could be copied by machines soon made it uneconomic for traders to deal in it (fig. 80).

The Exhibition brought in the golden silk bobbin laces of Malta, popular since the 1830s when they began to replace the lighter-weight French blondes. Now, the East Midlands attempted to compete, with the production of Beds Maltese (fig. 81), the guipure construction of which made it not only quicker to produce, but far more striking to wear, than Bucks point. For a time even professionals were employed to create this new and

80 *A flounce of Bucks point lace for a Court train, commissioned by Caroline, wife of the third Duke of Buckingham and Chandos c.1845. The 32-inch wide flounce is made of narrow strips joined together, and is 16 foot 4 inches long.*

81 *(below left) A fichu of spotted net banded and edged with Cluny, a guipure lace, made either in the East Midlands (Beds) or in central France (Le Puy), c.1860.*

82 *(a) The huge crinoline bears great yardage of lace, either patterned on the machine, or of plain net embroidered. 1859.*

82 *(b) A superb black shawl of Pusher lace patterned on the machine. The design echoes that of Paisley shawls, also popular during the crinoline period. Radius 46 inches, slightly deeper at the back. c.1860.*

(a)

(b)

83 (a) Below: a design for broderie anglaise drawn in ink on paper; above: the work completed in Madeira.

(b) The broderie anglaise on show. 'Pyramus and Thisbe', by William Maw Egly, 1861.

exciting lace, under the watchful eye of Thomas Lester of Bedford (1834–1909) who drew original designs for special commissions and won medals at the London Exhibitions of 1862 and 1872, the Paris Exhibition of 1867, and that of Vienna in 1873. Unfortunately for the English lace-makers the stimulus to new endeavours was not restricted to English shores. In France, the lace-makers of Le Puy, numbering then some 50,000, with their own fine designers, were creating similar guipures, at least as pretty, as closely textured, and as excellently wrought as those of Lester, but frequently using black silk instead of white linen thread.

In northern France the manufactories of Bayeux were also enjoying prosperity, as were those of Belgium. Beautiful capes and shawls of black Chantilly and white Brussels laces with their opulent floral designs, hung over the wide skirts like patterned cobwebs – sometimes disastrously, for now the tiny figure at the centre of the huge crinoline could scarcely know what her circumference was doing, and there was a danger of being roasted alive as flames from an open fire leapt through the filmy flounces (fig. 82). Brussels hand-made laces were now rising to a dominant position, maintaining an edge over less 'recherché laces' by

84 *An opulent version of renaissance lace. The convoluted machine-made tape is oversewn with pearls, the enclosed centres filled with buttonhole stitches. c.1895.*

the use of 'the finest flax thread grown at Hal and Rebecque'.

In 1853, Napoleon III married Eugénie, Countess of Montijo. She was to reinstate France as the leader of fashion and, in the process, to establish the world of the couturier as an exclusive replacement for that formerly exclusive, but now – caught in the crossfire between imperialism and democracy – rapidly disintegrating haute couture of the Court.

Paris had its own International Exhibition in 1855, and the Empress Eugénie wore for the prize-giving a dress of cherry-coloured velvet, its crinoline skirt entirely covered with Alençon needle lace, which had cost some 25,000 gold francs.[8] A more modest flounce and garniture, exhibited in London in 1851, had become part of Eugénie's trousseau. It had been worked by a great division of labour, as Queen Victoria's wedding lace had been, occupying 36 women over an 18-month period, and costing 22,000 francs. Eighteen months for approximately 22 days at eight hours a day gives a total of 114,000 working hours, or 3,166 hours per worker. Without knowing the amount of profit taken by the merchant, or the total cost of the thread (a fine linen worth per pound weight between £100 and £120), and the design (engraved on copper and printed in sections to be handed out to the workers), it is impossible to

do an accurate computation, but 22,000 francs was approximately £962.50 in the exchange rate of the time. Divided by 36, the rate for each worker becomes an absolute maximum of £26 for the 18 months, or £1.44 a month, or £0.36 a week. Imprecise as this calculation must be, the final figure nevertheless corresponds quite closely with the amount which hard-working Devon lace-makers might expect. 'The earnings of Honiton lace makers have been, during the last 4 years, on an excellent scale,' said a writer of the late 1850s, 'an average worker receiving upwards of 7s a week for 10 hours labour each day. . . .'[9]

The 1851 Exhibition had another side effect, in the publication in 1852 of a large volume entitled *The Illustrated Exhibitor*. Bursting with information on every conceivable topic of art, literature and general knowledge, it included numerous pages of instruction for the making of muslin appliqués after the manner of Carrickmacross; or the silk appliqué edged with chain-stitching on a coarse net; darned or tamboured nets; broderie anglaise or Madeira work (fig. 83); and that epitome of the meretricious imitation so characteristic of the period, the renaissance (point, tape, braid) lace based in the broadest possible manner on the sinuously flowing Milanese laces of the seventeenth and early eighteenth centuries (fig. 84).

These ideas were aimed at less prosperous readers, and at everyday wear rather than high fashion, but they meant that almost everyone, if they were prepared to make it, could wear lace.

85 *A fall cap, or fascinator. The centre of the straight edge rests above the forehead, the obtuse point faces backwards, the side flaps are called ear-pieces, or lappets. Made on the Pusher machine, c.1870.*

The heavier forms of craft lace became parasol covers, cravats, jabots, mandarin cuffs, collars, and that perennially popular accessory of the mid-nineteenth century, the fall cap. This was the democratized version of the lace cap and lappets of Court, which were now themselves giving way to veils of variable length surmounted by ostrich feather plumes, and which had derived originally from the headdresses of servants in early Tudor times (figs 85, 147).

The 1860s

The boisterous fashions of the prosperous 1850s were sobered by two events in the early 1860s: the outbreak of the American Civil War (1861–5) which closed for a time a profitable export market, and the death of Prince Albert in 1861 which plunged Victoria and Victorian England into a profound period of mourning. This latter, as far as fashion was concerned, benefited no one but the machine manufacturers, for machines, being eyeless, suffered no pain in their production of black laces, and could disgorge them in all shapes, sizes, designs and textures, by the ton.

In Paris, in the early 1860s, the Empress Eugénie met the still young couturier Worth, and between them they conspired to bring about a revolution in fashion. He, hating the ostentation of the crinoline, designed a dress of shapely elegance, smooth across the front, and with the skirt draped up at the back to fall into sinuously frilled folds like the lissom tail of

a mermaid (fig. 86). Somewhat in the manner of Rose Bertin and Marie Antoinette in the eighteenth century, Worth and the Empress over the next few years egged each other on to perpetually new creations. Worth's 'simplicities' were extremely expensive. 'It will cost me the earth,' wrote Madame Feuillet to her old nurse, describing a gown she had ordered at short notice, which was of lilac silk covered with clouds of matching tulle in which clusters of lilies-of-the-valley sank and drowned, the whole overhung with a veil of white net, like a mist, and finished with a flowing sash suggesting in Worth's own words 'the reins of Venus' chariot'. 'With the money I'm squandering here,' she continued complacently, 'I could have bought you a little house for your old age'.[10]

Napoleon III managed to justify his wife's extravagance in much the same way as Charles II had done his own: the purchases would provide examples which poorer people could copy. Napoleon added his own optimistic philosophy that the greater the expenditure of the rich, the greater would be the incomes of the poor. But in this he was as out of touch with reality as Henri IV, first Bourbon king of France, who amiably wanted everyone to eat chicken on Sundays.[11] The poor remained unimpressed and, ultimately, antagonistic.

The indefatigable Mrs Beeton of *The Englishwoman's Domestic Magazine*, which was edited by her husband Samuel, regularly visited Paris to bring back little gems of gossip, as well as reports on the latest fashions. In December 1868 her successor, the 'Silkworm' visited the exhibition at Le Havre, and her column bubbled with enthusiasm about dresses 'shaped in the prevailing style', which we learn is 'Watteau', and looking 'exquisite over moire or satin jupons'. They were of 'Brussels point, point de gaze and Chantilly laces. . . . It is *la*

mode to have dress, mouchoir and lappets to correspond, and lace costumes are, like jewellery, made *en suite*.' She also saw 'Spanish Chantilly mantillas, fitted for *sortie de bal* or *voile espagnole*', or made into beautiful deep collars, or exquisite lace flounces, shawls, and exciting mantelets nipped in at the waist before spreading out gracefully over the hips.

The broderie anglaise promoted by *The Illustrated Exhibitor* of 1852, for semi-leisured ladies to make, was in the 1860s being imitated on a commercial scale by the 'hand machine' or 'hand embroidery machine' developed from the 1820s' invention of Joshua Heilmann in Switzerland, and slowly perfected until it could convincingly imitate any needlework stitch, including buttonhole stitch, but not the knot. Heilmann's invention had been patented in England by Bock, and the rights bought by the Manchester firm of Henry Houldsworth in 1829. Illustrations in *The Englishwoman's Domestic Magazine* show this 'Swiss embroidery' mainly on children's clothes, ladies' underwear, or maids' aprons, but occasionally the simpler day dresses of the demi-fashionable might sport it as 'lingerie', that is visible chemisettes, underblouses and neckties. Some finely detailed collars of open whitework, similar to Appenzal embroidery, were made on these machines by the Iklé family of St Gallen in Switzerland (fig. 87).

86 *(a) The post-crinoline fashion, designed by Worth.*
(b) Detail of the beautiful tail which swished along the floor, protected by a dust ruffle of crimped cotton and stiffened machine lace. c.1870.

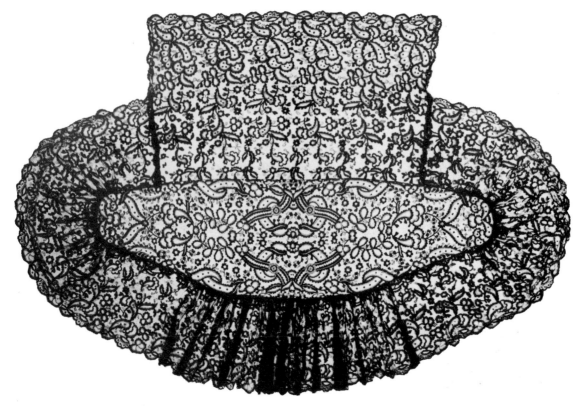

87 *Two whitework collars and a pair of cuffs, which might have been embroidered by hand, or made on the hand machine. Ex Jacoby collection, 1860s.*

88 *A traditional Spanish mantilla of silk bobbin lace, black blonde. The rectangle would rise over the tall comb, and the flounced oval would be wrapped around the shoulders and crossed at the front. Mid-nineteenth century, or earlier.*

Hand-made laces, though subdued, were not dead. Bayeux continued to produce its illustrious exhibition pieces, such as the Alençon dress shown at the Paris Exhibition of 1867, which cost 85,000 francs (equivalent to £3,400 in that year) and which had taken 40 women seven years to complete. Craft laces also continued, though they depended very much on charitable patronage. Miss Pedder's School, in Tipperary, for the Employment of Industrious Poor Cottage Women, was producing in 1874 'crochet caps in beautiful old point guipure, Greek lace parasol covers, lappets of English point lace work, and tatting edging for pinafores at 8s 6d [42½p] for 12 yards.'

The 1870s

1870 saw further political upheavals in France. Napoleon III, misguidedly attacking Prussia, whose strength he had underestimated, was taken prisoner with 80,000 of his men. Eugénie fled to England where, in 1871, Napoleon joined her and, two years later, died. Eugénie herself crept, like Victoria, into black retirement. But Worth carried on, becoming ever more the darling of the Americans, whom he loved in return because they had 'faith, figures and francs'.[12] Real princesses, especially those of expatriate monarchies, now most often wore quite ordinary clothes, and travelled on public transport – horse-drawn omnibuses were established in France in the 1830s. Worth, though he could not be bought by money alone, was yet content to satisfy, at vast expense, the pride and vanity of any society lady rich enough, or pretentious enough, to care.

But the glorious radiance of the Second Empire was extinguished, and the rapturous glow of Worth's earlier creations could not be recaptured. His gentle serpentine bustles were hardened by the end of the decade into projecting slabs carried behind like the tray of a highchair awkwardly draped. That stolidity which was never far from the Victorian scene loomed like a tired middle-agedness to cramp the ladies' walk, and stiffen their posture. The prolific laces fell over the dresses in cascades as dull and heavy as weed-ridden waterfalls. Worth's son Jean, studying the dress of Alexandra, Princess of Wales, on the occasion of the Paris Exhibition of 1878, thought it laboriously elaborate. With a great flounce of lace across the skirt and the awkward Court train she looked 'for all the world like a maid decked out in her mistress's cast-off finery on her afternoon off.'[13]

The age of sentimentality and romanticism had passed, and a new determination was in the air, an upsurge of feminism (then known as 'womanism') which chilled the externals of women along with their hearts, and made even the clothes they wore look militant.

Magazines gave space to heated arguments on women's rights, and suffrage; as well as to deplorings of the increase in elaboration of dress which now included endless bouillons (puffed folds) of tulle, as in 'a plastron of bouilloné maize tulle ornamented with leaves of maroon velvet; a dress of white tulle designed in bouillons over white silk with a long fringe of flowers over the skirt recalling certain toilets of the court of Versailles in the time of Louis Quatorze.' Yet they revelled in descriptions of the latest modes in the jargon of the time: 'Among the pretty *nouveautés* are a number of elegant *gilets*. One of the most tasteful is the Joan of Arc *cuirasse* of white *rep de chine*, with ruffle of Mechlin lace or point d'Alençon round the neck; and the Pompadour, of white lace with light blue- and rose-coloured bows.'

Other laces mentioned are Chantilly, especially on hats; guipure lace, edging a casaque of marine-blue cashmere; and a *mantelet écharpe* (shawl mantle) of black cashmere trimmed with 'black guipure lace put on all round the edge and down the middle of the back *en cascade*, or of black silk trimmed with deep Chantilly lace or with black Spanish blond beaded with jet' (see fig. 88). Dinner dresses were not now fully décolleté, the corsage being open just in the shape of a heart or a square with a 'tulle ruche, or a drapery formed of tulle and edged with Mechlin or point lace'.

As to the identity of the Mechlin, point, guipure, Chantilly, Spanish blond, and 'white' laces which are mentioned, we are left guessing. Hand or machine? Bobbin, needle or craft? Each name had at least two meanings, and we can draw no firm conclusions as to origin or even technique, and only tentative ones as to texture and design.

The Englishwoman's Domestic Magazine also reviewed the book *Antique Point and Honiton Lace*, written by Mrs Treadwin: 'Amongst the higher class of society, Mrs Treadwin, of Exeter, is considered the high priestess of the art of lace-making; and the number of bridal veils which she has designed for the sweet English girls of the aristocracy would form a goodly sum in every way.' The book, published in 1874, included a section on colouring lace to give it an 'antique tint'. This quaint custom arose no doubt from 'the fixed clear desire on the part of everyone who loves refinement in dress to have some good lace in her possession.' (*E.D.M.* April 1873.) To *know* that one has is one thing, but how can one *show* that one has? The antique linen laces had always a faint nuance of off-whiteness about them. Hallowed by time, the infinitesimal greyness became a pale discoloured ivory, and it was this which aroused awe and envy in all who saw it.

New hand-made cotton laces, on the other hand, were not discoloured, but brightly white; and machine laces in their 'grey' or 'brown' state, full of oil and stains, had to be boiled, bleached, stretched and stiffened before appearing startlingly clean on the retailer's shelf. Mrs Treadwin's instructions for producing the desirable 'écru' were to infuse a quarter-pound of 'the very best coffee', strain it, and throw it over the lace until the colour 'imitates that of pure unbleached linen thread'. Alas, such a subtle change was no good at all in these heavy-handed times. The vigorous boiling in coffee to which the lace was in consequence subjected produced not so much an antique tint as a kind of earthy mud. 'It is not in good taste' came the inevitable querulous comment 'to affect the colour Isabeau, in plain English the colour of dirt.'

The indomitable ladies with their 'rage for lace, old or new', were even less to be trusted with 'lace, old'. Value it they might, but it had to fit into the current fashion. Thus antique lappets were joined to make ties or scarves, machine picot borders were added to eighteenth-century pieces to give them the right *ton*, damaged pieces were dissected and re-grounded even though it ruined the design and the new mesh was inappropriate, while magnificent ecclesiastical flounces of the seventeenth century were cut like yardages of material to get out matching collars, cuffs and edgings. Mrs Treadwin capped it all with her 1873 advertisement for 'New mediaeval laces: specimens sent on approval' (fig. 89).[14]

The 1880s

Excesses continued to proliferate in the following years, and the purveyors of good taste found no listeners among the rich. Industrial tycoons bought titles for themselves and their families. Their wives had no need to be 'ladylike': they were themselves

89 *The new mediaeval laces, made of braid with minimal hand-stitching.* The Young Ladies' Journal, *1877.*

the new aristocracy, developing their own elaborate and exclusive *mores* in which money – the ultimate hypocrisy – was never mentioned.

Bustles, or tournures, went suddenly, so that skirts dropped round the legs, trussing them into a mincing hobble until the fashionable lady was barely able to move her feet six inches at a time. Dead birds and other fauna returned, as if whole gardens of blossom were not enough. Hats piled high with white wings ripped from innumerable doves could be regarded as 'chaste' symbols of innocence, and the grotesque comment 'it would be better taste to wear only two or three as half a dozen is the average now chosen' seems tainted with madness. Fifty million humming birds were slaughtered annually to provide an iridescent aura, or to be stuffed and stuck into mountains of false hair from which unfamiliar environ they peered out glassily, their tails raised and studded with diamonds. Compared with those monstrosities lace itself had a kind of purity, even though its makers were badly treated. It was in its way a work of art, and all the rest no more than cruel and disharmonious accretions.

Fashions were yet again surpassing themselves and getting out of hand. There was constant change, irrational complexity, agitation, confusion, unbearable weights (14 to 20 lb of clothes), impossible constrictions. Men, in contrast, were becoming soberer, stuffier, drabber, until any man in the least showily dressed was *ipso facto* a snob, a cad or a bounder.

The only women to dress quite plainly were the

3 Sir Henry Oxenden. By Thomas Hudson, *c*.1756. The cravat is becoming a plain linen stock. The chitterling and ruffles, with their rich floral design, could be Brussels bobbin lace of the type known as point d'Angleterre, or the sort of drawnwork illustrated in fig. 53c. The hat is trimmed with silver lace.

4 A portrait by James Hayllar of his young daughter, and a friend, *c*.1866. She wears a broderie anglaise dress, at that time becoming so short that 'it scarcely covers the child's back when she bends down' as a correspondent in a contemporary magazine complained.

rare followers of the Aesthetic Movement promoted by William Morris and Burne-Jones, and of the pre-Raphaelite Brotherhood promoted by Holman Hunt and Rossetti. The aim was to return to natural lines, a figure without distortions, and clothes without clutter. If they ever wore lace, it was sparse and incidental, and not connected with fashion (fig. 90).

Hand-made laces were losing the economic battle even before the nineteenth century ended. Some of the few centres still to flourish were those of Belgium, namely Brussels, Bruges, Ypres and Ghent, the latter two now making Valenciennes. Brussels laces were of a variety of techniques, from bobbin Duchesse to needle lace point de gaze; also tambour embroidery on net; and bobbin, needle or muslin appliqués. All showed an opulent full-blown beauty organized into a harmonious if somewhat busy design.

A superb wedding veil of Brussels point de gaze, constructed entirely of buttonhole stitches in a very fine cotton, was made by Leon Sacré for Stephanie, daughter of King Leopold II of Belgium, when she married the Crown Prince Rudolf of Austria in 1881. The union ended tragically barely a year later when Rudolf and his young mistress Maria Vetsera committed suicide in the hunting lodge at Mayerling, near Vienna.

The Bruges flower laces, similar in technique to those of Brussels, differed in their clean, fresh, bold appearance as opposed to the overpowering richness of the Brussels lace. They were popular as yokes, choker collars and berthas, and were to become even more fashionable in the 1890s. In England, these highly professional imported laces sold for little more than the country-style laces made in the cottages around Honiton. This state of affairs brought an acid protest from Penderell Moody, of the Revival Lace School, Lower Sloane Street, as to 'the unscrupulous sweating so rife in Belgium' and the nuns who, 'by the help of their unpaid workers [children, nominally apprentices] have undertaken orders at prices that would mean starvation to a woman solely dependent on her earnings.'[15] (Fig. 91.)

An attempt to boost Bucks laces was made in 1884 at the International Health Exhibition when Peter Robinson published a booklet entitled *Buckingham Lace* which showed charming designs to be ordered through a Mr Viccars. Beds laces, as well, never ceased to play their small part, in low rather than high fashion, but whatever greater success they might have achieved was negated by a new development in the late 1880s, the adaptation of the Schiffli embroidery machine to produce laces.

90 *Dress of the Pre-Raphaelite movement, reminiscent of the Creole style of the late eighteenth century. The lace at the neck and sleeves is independent of fashion. 'The School of Nature', by William Holman Hunt, 1893.*

The Schiffli, developed in Switzerland, differed from the hand embroidery machine in using two sets of threads, needle and shuttle; also in its commonest stitches, known as blatt and steil, being unlike any made by hand. It was versatile: by embroidery on net it gave the impression of a meshed or reseaud lace, and could imitate the appearance of point de gaze designs; by embroidery on a fabric which was later destroyed leaving only the closely compacted embroidery stitches, it produced a lace of the guipure type with the design-elements linked by bars, and thus it copied the fashionable Duchesse, Brussels Rosaline and Irish crochet. The destructive principle which got rid of the fabric was chemical corrosion, and this gave rise to the popular name 'chemical', 'burnt' or 'burnt-out' laces. Their trade name was 'Swiss-embroidered guipure laces', which was soon abbreviated to 'guipures', to our later confusion. Now, they are mainly called 'Swiss laces'.

91 *A magnificent flounce of bobbin lace, combining the finest qualities of Belgian design with decorative fillings from early eighteenth-century Flemish laces, and leadworks from Devon. The geographical origin is uncertain. Second half of the nineteenth century.*

Though these laces, closely examined, appeared fuzzy and not at all pleasing, they were a fashion triumph. They could be produced as all-over patterned yardages, or as bands of edgings. If they were cut and rejoined after leaving the machine, they could be made into shaped pieces such as collars and godets (fig. 92). From a few feet away they could give the impression of some of the most beautiful hand laces that ever existed.

There could scarcely have been a greater advantage in a society sufficiently unsure of itself to need strong and unmistakable signals. A dress loaded with ornament was now regarded as a sign of wealth, a lace striking the eye from across the room as a sign of quality, a man dressed in a severe and soberly laceless suit as a sign of worthiness. Child-like, didactic and ignorant though this attitude may have been, yet it ruled society, society ruled fashion, and fashion ruled lace.

The 1890s

By the 1890s chemical laces were dominating all others. It was in this close-of-the-century period that the militancy of female dress reached its most aggressive phase. The choker collar, said to have been introduced by Princess Alexandra to hide a scar on her throat, rose higher, like the top of a guardsman's tunic. The protruberant bust, the nipped-in waist, and the prominent bottom gave an S-shaped profile bearing a striking resemblance to a wooden toy soldier. The impression was reinforced by the broad shoulders and narrow hips of tailored suits and evening gowns alike. The latter were now near-topless, the bare chest and back framed with obtrusive lace flounces which rose majestically above short sleeves puffed out like balloons (fig. 93).

Lace frothed everywhere, forming even entire dresses, yet with no more femininity than the bifurcated bicycling suits deplored by Monsieur Hénon as threatening that essential delicacy of the female sex which only lace could bestow (but then as a lace manufacturer he was not entirely impartial).

The success of the Schiffli offered severe competition to the Leavers machine, which was capable of infinitely superior designs and textures (fig. 94), but was hampered by its own complexities of construction, slowness of setting up, and expense both of patterning and of the highly skilled labour required. However, in novelty hat-veilings Leavers had the advantage. These veils were fixed to the crowns of the large hats and tied under the chin, and all kinds and colours were produced in great quantity. Spotted nets were particularly in demand, and a

92 *The handkerchief border is a good imitation of Brussels Rosaline bobbin lace, but is made on the Schiffli machine, 1890s.*

93 *The huge shoulders and high military collars of these aggressively lacy blouses give a tremendous visual impact in which the technique of the lace is insignificant. Woolland Brothers of Knightsbridge, 1897.*

94 *The lace leaf of this 1890s' fan shows the delicate and beautiful designs of which the Leavers machine was capable: only the utmost skill of both draughtsman and twist hands could produce such complex symmetry.*

95 *A real tambour lace scarf, tied in a bow beneath the chin; also examples of Malines and Bretonne laces; and a dainty waistcoat trimmed with butter-coloured lace. Dickens and Jones, 1897.*

chenilling device patented in Nottingham at the turn of the century could produce chenille spotted veiling at the rate of 190,000 spots an hour.[16] But the technique was expensive, and cheaper imitations were made by glueing furry dollops of soot to black net, so that it was no wonder that black veils were said to 'redden the eyes and harm the complexion'.

The gaudy fashion for elaborate icings of lace festooned over gowns persisted throughout the decade. 'This is a season in which lace reigns predominant,' said a writer in 1897, 'dresses and skirts are made of it, it appears as trimmings to nearly all the smartest summer gowns, lace scarves are among the prevailing modes.'[17] (Fig. 95.)

While some of these scarves, or stoles, were of white or écru net embroidered by the Cornely machine to resemble Brussels tambour, others were produced on the Pusher machine. This had reached its peak in the crinoline period, with its great lama shawls of mohair, and splendid imitations of Chantilly. After the collapse of the crinoline in the late 1860s, it turned to shiny copies of Spanish blondes, in black or pale cream. They were made mostly at Lyons, and their production continued into the early 1900s.

5
The Twentieth Century
THE END OF FASHION AS DEFINED

The fashions of the late nineteenth century lingered on into the early twentieth, as though a kind of inertia kept them from perceiving that the counting away of yet another hundred years had begun. In the seventeenth, eighteenth and nineteenth centuries a whole quiescent decade had been allowed to slip by before any major changes were set in motion, but in the twentieth century the situation was a little different, for exclusive couturiers, following Worth's example, had incessantly to promote that constant change upon which their splendid incomes depended. The result was styles as *outré* and impractical as any known to Courts of the past, so that a chasm was created between haute couture and normal living as deep and near-impassable as had separated those far-off royalties from the common people.

1900–1910

For France this decade was part of 'La Belle Epoque'. Paris led the fashions with designers such as Doucet, Poiret and Paquin. As, under their influence, nineteenth-century styles faded away, so lace, having survived the vicissitudes of almost 400 years, began at last to become *démodé*.

During the first few years, however, it continued to flourish. Pouched bodices had dog collars of chemical lace guipure (fig. 96), Irish crochet or Maltese – though an article in *The Times* in 1904 reported that the quality of Maltese 'has fallen off lately, Messrs Dickens and Jones find that they cannot depend on it'. Transparent 'pneumonia blouses' of lace and muslin, or lace and chiffon, were popular, and silk bobbinets were used for cravats tied round the neck in a bow which drooped like a jabot. Large lace fans supplanted lace handkerchiefs for evening wear, and were themselves discarded in 1914. Old ladies might still wear frilly lace caps indoors, but only because they clung to the past. Parasols were long-handled and often covered in lace. Patterned machine laces continued to enjoy an upward trend, still eagerly bought by those who

could not afford 'real' laces, still having a disastrous effect on the traders in those real laces who badgered the makers into turning out lace as quickly and cheaply as possible with the result that it was often bad and nobody wanted it.

Good laces found it almost impossible to compete commercially. The beautiful Irish needle lace, Youghal, made in County Cork, was kept going by royal commissions for a while, and a fan leaf was

96 *Summer toilette. A blue foulard dress with guipure on the revers, sleeves and skirt. The rosette of muslin has lace ends, the white pique vest two rows of lace, and the tall parasol is also lace-trimmed.* The Graphic, *June 1900.*

97 *An all-over lace design created for the Leavers machine, first quarter of the twentieth century.*

98 *An art nouveau collar and handkerchief, from the Imperial Central School of Lace-making in Vienna, c.1902.*

ordered for the wedding of Princess Maud of Wales, daughter of Edward VII, to the Crown Prince of Denmark in 1896; but soon after 1900 it ceased production.

Others were not immediately left to die. Investigative committees sought to focus attention on the distressed condition of English lace-makers. Lace schools were founded in the East Midlands by Princess Christina, mother of Queen Alexandra, and by Princess Mary of Wales, wife of the future George V. But in spite of royal patronage, innumerable begging letters to members of the aristocracy, and the well sponsored work of the North Bucks Lace Association which managed to increase the work force of lace-makers from 300 in 1905 to 1,800 in 1911, and to deposit their productions along the shelves of the lace departments in London stores, the anachronistic naïvety of Bucks laces was inevitably outmoded by the 'new art' which expressed itself in imaginative machine designs of gliding swallows, spiders straddling their delicate webs, dragonflies among bullrushes, puffing railway engines, and soaring hot air balloons. At the Brussels International Exhibition of 1910 were shown 'the first really artistic original works which raised machine lace to the level of that made by hand.'[1] This development in machine laces followed a logical sequence: hand-made laces no longer had prestige appeal, therefore it was no advantage to have the machines copy them (fig. 97).

Non-commercial schools, funded by government grants, were set up in other European countries to make very high quality laces which, being produced only in small amounts, and being too expensive to compete with other laces, could not be worn prolifically enough to provide that essential *sine qua non* of fashion as originally defined – a mode of life. Students at the Imperial Central School of Lace-making in Vienna made lovely art nouveau collars (fig. 98); the Kantcentrum in Bruges (formerly the School of the Apostoline Sisters) delightful handkerchiefs bordered with a form of Binche known as 'point de fée' (fig. 99); the Scuola di Merletti in Burano superb copies of seventeenth-century needle laces of Venice and elsewhere; the Lefebure firm in Bayeux some fine eighteenth-century Argentan; and the Aemilia Ars Society of Bologna excellent copies of sixteenth-century needle laces from the 1591 pattern book of Passarotti. Burano also produced, commercially, the needle lace Alençon, formerly made in France (*The Times* 1904).

All the above, except the last, were well beyond the world of fashion which, for a few years, still continued the militant body line, the gored skirt enlarged at the hem with godets, and the bodice smothered in braids, frills and flounces which had all the stiff intractability of elaborately carved sandalwood.

1910—1920

The first item to succumb to the general slackening of dress after 1910 was the stiffened collar which, stripped away, left a round or slightly V-shaped neckline decorated with a little Peter Pan collar (named after James Barrie's play, first performed in 1904). The shocking appearance of bare skin in the daytime was hastily covered with a little modesty or chemisette; but such coyness was short-lived, and soon quite deeply square necklines were socially acceptable and large cape-, sailor- or fichu-collars, sometimes entirely of lace, accompanied them.

As corsets became softer and eased their pressure, the ramrod backs relaxed a little, making possible a less armoured body line, but the tightness fell down the legs and women were hobbled in skirts little

more, at ankle level, than a yard in circumference (1912—14). The waist began to resume its normal size and, to conceal the change, dresses became themselves straighter, or were covered with loose tunics of filet or Irish crochet, sometimes open and coming to a tasselled point at the front or sides (fig. 100).

In these dresses, sleeves were also relaxed, draping over the shoulder without a seam, in Magyar style, reflecting an Eastern influence, no doubt derived from interest aroused by the Boxer Rebellion of 1900—1, the Russo-Japanese War of 1904—5, and the arrival in Paris of Diaghilev's *Ballets Russes* in 1909. The filet which banded the dresses of cotton or silk, and sometimes made up entire jackets or blouses, had enjoyed a revival in France and Italy during the last quarter of the nineteenth century. It was also popularly known as lacis, opus araneum, point conté, filet brodé, punto a maglia quadra and modano – among others.[2] European filets were usually made of linen thread,

99 *A handkerchief border of point de fée, 2½ inches deep. Bruges, first quarter of the twentieth century.*

100 *The straighter body line, with less lace.*

(a) A layered dress, with broderie anglaise openwork (Schiffli), narrows at the ankles into a hobbled skirt; the Magyar sleeves come smoothly off the shoulders, and the neckline is round, leaving the throat bare.

(b) A large lace collar and jabot of spotted net.

(c) A Peter Pan collar.

(d) The tunic, and square collar.

(e) A fichu.

(f) A Bretelle. All 1910–12

importations from China of cotton. They were also copied, patterned or plain, on the Lace Curtain machine, from about 1870.

For evening wear, gold and silver machine laces were popular, and evening scarves were of gauze or tulle. Black or white mittens were still worn, though not for much longer. As the skirts lifted a little and stockings became visible, their fronts were decorated with lace insets, some of very fine quality such as black Chantilly, or Alençon dyed a pinky-beige (fig. 101). These cost 8s 6d a pair in 1912, but less expensive forms decorated with openwork knitting could be obtained. Little capes of lace might be worn indoors and, outdoors, huge hats tied on with novelty veiling, made mostly by machine, but some by hand in the East Midlands using horse hair and tinsel.

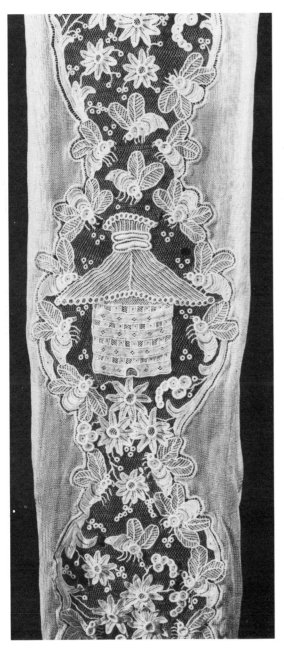

101 *Lace stocking fronts. An inset of Alençon needle lace decorated with bees,* c.*1912.*

102 *A wedding veil of Brussels mixed bobbin and needle lace appliqué on net, detail.* c.*1915.*

1920–1939

It is not easy to discover the precise position which lace held in popular favour during this period. The grim war years of 1914–18, with their total casualties (killed, wounded, prisoners and missing) of over 37 million, had left their mark on fashion. The town of Ypres and all the surrounding flax-growing areas had been destroyed. England, after the war, had a trade agreement with Belgium to supply thread in return for lace. These laces had somehow to be absorbed in wear. Thus point de gaze, Duchesse and Bruges were available, albeit in simple and reduced forms, and they tended to be just a trimming which could as well be replaced by another kind.

Though it might still be true, as it had been 16 years earlier, that 'when it is possible to obtain old lace, this is always worn in preference to any modern creation', and that 'for everyday wear imitation lace is generally preferred, but there are some occasions when every woman desires to experience that satisfaction which comes from wearing real lace', the whole world might well have felt far less certain of anything, even of whether real or imitation in fact mattered very much.

This indecision, the confrontation, as it were, of fantasy and reality, seems epitomized in fig. 103, where the lady's gauche upper part with its ped-

For all except the most noble marriages, when Honiton or Brussels (fig. 102) was preferred, wedding veils were fairly plain, of silk tulle lightly embroidered with silver thread, in chain stitch worked by hand or by the Cornely machine.

An attractive variation was the stencilling of lace patterns in gold on dark velvet by the designer Fortuny, *c.*1912.

WHENAS IN SILKS MY JULIA GOES
THEN, THEN (METHINKS) HOW SWEETLY FLOWS
THAT LIQUEFACTION OF HER CLOTHES   *Herrick.*

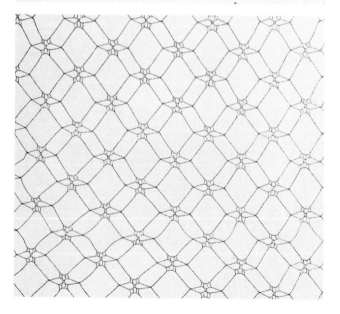

103 *The waistline has dropped a little, the skirt lifted. The filmy lace flounce is patterned all over, and cut like a dress fabric. c.1920.*

104 *A motoring veil of fancy net, detail. Early twentieth century.*

105 *(opposite) (a) A boudoir cap, 1915.*
(b) A light gown of patterned voile, the deep V-neck filled with a modesty which could be decorated with openwork embroidery.
(c) A blouse of chocolate brown taffeta with a revered collar of gold, or multi-coloured silk, embroidered lace. c.1920.
(d) An evening dress, the skirt, shoulder straps and 'wing' sleeves of machine lace, the bodice and the weighted skirt-points of satin. 1922.
(e) A hat veil, 1920.
(f) An afternoon frock in brown velvet 'trimmed with good lace', 1933.
(g) A blouse with embroidered lace.
(h) A wedding dress with lace bertha and net veil, 1958.

estrian hat strives to instil some lyricism into her filmy lace flounces. Herrick's verse, quoted below the photograph, jars sadly with this untimely image. His lines *Upon Julia's Clothes* had all the outspoken directness and childlike insouciance of the seventeenth-century extrovert: 'Fain would I kiss my Julia's dainty leg, Which is as white and hairless as an egg' (*On Julia's Legs*, Herrick, 1591–1674). The 1920s were too old for such innocence.

The Leavers machine had recovered sufficiently from the reeling blow of that unproductive period to be able to manufacture light-hearted lightweight all-over yardages which could be made up into dresses. However they were no longer the extremely complex designs of the 1850s and '60s. Those required skills which had already been lost, and hand-finishing which was already too expensive.

At Liberty's lace exhibition in 1926 the catalogue proclaimed, 'the fashion for beautiful lace is on the eve of return.' It was an appointment which was never kept. London was now almost devoid of 'lacemen', retaining only two or three to deal with the requirements of family occasions such as weddings and baptisms.

The fancy motoring and hat veils (fig. 104) of the first decade were becoming transformed into func-

(a)

(b)

(c)

(d)

(e)

(f)

(g)

(h)

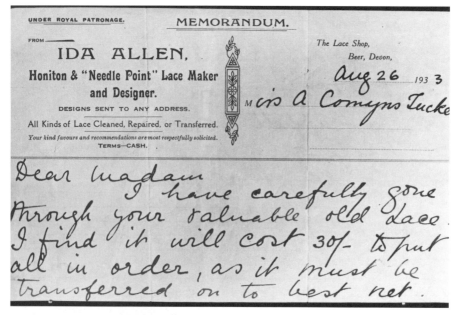

106 (a) *Part of a letter from Ida Allen to a customer, 1933.*

(b) *A white embroidery on muslin being 'transferred to best net'. The battered piece has been first tacked down (on the right), then each leaflet and petal closely stitched on to the net, and finally all excess material cut away (on left).*

tional objects such as hair nets. In June 1928 the *Empire Mail*[3] reported:

> Although it might be imagined that trade in ladies' silk hair nets, fringe nets and bandeaux had fallen off considerably since bobbed or shingled hair became the vogue, such is not the case. *Tango* and *Hide and Seek* brands of hair net are so cleverly constructed as to be invisible in wear although effectively serving their purpose in maintaining the wave of the hair [permanent waving began in 1904]. The *Halo* range of sleeping and boudoir caps are in delicate pastel shades.

These romantic little boudoir caps with their pretty silk ribbons and machine lace frills were part of the gushy, almost novelettish, attitude of advertisers, the whole tenor of whose pronouncements was that no girl had a hope of success in her private or public life unless she was simply 'slathered' (their word) in lace (fig. 142). They were attempting to convey an unreal image of the romance of lace. In fact nothing could be further from the truth. Romance is by definition a fiction or wish-fulfilment. Lace, as a fabric, had never been romantic: the realities of its existence were hard work, skill, money and status. The plight of the people who made the laces, right through the centuries, had been one of extreme distress most of the time. They worked incredibly long hours, they were extremely badly paid, they were cheated by merchants. The people who wore the lace were for the most part vain, arrogant, egotistical and proud. Perhaps they appreciated the artistry of the lace, but it seems rather more likely that it was simply a symbol made use of, through a 300-year period, to inflate their visible importance.

107 *A bouffant evening gown of nylon lace, in almond green over layers of pink tulle, c.1950. All-overs were made in preference to edgings at this time.*

In the stark post-war reality of the early '20s, these meretricious promotions were of no avail. Lace was playing a progressively inferior part. Its appearances, for special occasions, were relatively rare, and not strictly lace in fashion. Small collars and matching cuffs in silk or rayon decorated with openwork embroidery from the Schiffli machine, or modesties filling in steeply slanted V-necks, were almost all there was, though the art deco period brought with it some beautifully patterned machine lace shawls with brilliant designs in bronze, orange, dark brown and gold (see fig. 105).

A fresh aspect of lace in fashion was the screen-printing of laces onto silk, which made stunningly chic dresses. Also, a kind of photographic printing, in black on a plain ground, produced a striking *trompe l'oeil* effect of a lace overlay; while block-printing of simple shapes onto patterned machine laces brought the design into sharp relief within each area of colour. The idea was revived in the 1960s when a new method of heat-transfer printing onto milanese fabrics again produced a precise imitation of an actual lace, from a distance, though since multi-colour effects were often used, it was unlikely in fact to be taken for one.

As the '20s passed, and skirts edged their way higher up the legs, rising from 8 inches above the ground to 17 inches in 1928, the patterned machine laces, and the machine nets weighed down with thousands of hand-stitched beads, were being replaced by silk chiffons. 'One can walk down Oxford Street or Bond Street,' said a Heathcoat representative of this period, 'and hardly see a single lady wearing net in any form.'[4]

Jessie Caplin gives a picture of the hand and machine laces available about 1930. The hand were almost entirely Brussels, Bruges, Antwerp, or the Belgian form of Valenciennes. Many of the machine forms were named, for trade purposes, after hand-made laces to which they bore no resemblance whatsoever, for example Binche, Alençon, Mechlin and Chantilly from the Leavers machine, and Venise from the Schiffli. A few unscrapped Pusher machines were resurrected in Lyons as 'real old bobbinet machines', and put to making a 'hand run Alençon', that is a machine lace using the trade name Alençon, and having the pattern outlined by a coarse thread run in by hand.

Into the 1930s the Bucks Lace Making Industry, and others, continued to succour East Midlands lace-makers by charitable commissions. Shops such as that of Ida Allen of the Lace Shop, Beer, continued to clean, repair and transfer older lace, that is, to cut away the original ground and substitute another, usually of machine net (fig. 106). Mrs Treadwin's establishment in Exeter, under the management of Miss West, successor to Miss Herbert, did the same.

Thus lace, both old and new, was still circulating, though fashion drawings in the magazines of the time show remarkably little of it. Sleeveless evening gowns with deep V-backs were occasionally made of gold machine lace, Hollywood-style. On a more mundane level, hand-knitted lacy wool jumpers, dorothy bags of crochet worked in Sylko, and stockings with openwork clocks represented meagre sops to the wearing of lace. Indeed it is only by strict conformity to the *Oxford English Dictionary* definition that one can call them lace at all.

It was an uneasy time: the Wall Street crash of 1929, followed by the depression of 1932–3, had put factories themselves in distress. Vast amounts of capital were tied up in huge machines, and with the

108 *A glamorous gown by Marisa Martin, one of the first young designers to appreciate the fashion potential of nineteenth-century laces which were still, in the 1960s, looked down on as bearing no comparison with earlier forms. By the 1980s machine laces could be specially designed to imitate nineteenth-century originals, and create effects just as elegant. 1981.*

109 *A minidress of black machine lace, with a hood which covers the hair, worn with warp-knit tights which have a lacy pattern. Vogue, 1965.*

110 *Point de gaze, sometimes called Brussels point. Part of a flounce, 8 inches deep, c.1900. 'The choicest specimens are made in Convents by the Sisters. The finest cotton is used – the number varies from 150 to 500.' Quoted from a Belgian catalogue, c.1910.*

slackening of demand they were becoming uneconomic to run. The destructive Spanish Civil War of 1936–9, and the death from starvation of over two million people in the Ukraine consequent upon Stalin's collectivized farming policy, drew attention away from frilly decorations for body coverings, while the outbreak of the Second World War in 1939 drew away lace-makers and twist-hands for work of national importance such as making bombs.

1939 and on

By the end of the War in 1945, 'lace' for most people was a word which had become almost meaningless, except for its association with dowdiness, maiden aunts, crowded Victorian drawing rooms, and meaningless pieces hidden in museums. A lot was turned out and destroyed. New machine laces as dress fabrics had the sole advantage that no clothing coupons were needed to buy them. Thus they were made up into wide-skirted evening gowns which, though of ephemeral popularity, persisted through later decades as the established wear for competitions in ballroom dancing (fig. 107).

111 (a) The Princess of Wales' wedding gown arranged on a model to show the impressive sweep of the train and the filmy softness of the tulle illusion veil from Heathcoat's which lies over it. The pretty, yet formal, lace edging of Brussels-type design is a faithful copy of the dainty Carrickmacross, formerly the property of Queen Mary, which enriches the bodice and sleeves.

(b) Above, detail of the lace for the train; below, of the underskirt. Schiffli needlerun, designed and made by Roger Watson of Nottingham, 1981.

In spite of this discouraging attitude, in the 1950s two new machines were paving the way for a lace revival – the Barmen and the Raschel. Neither was entirely new. The Barmen, in the form of a braiding machine, had been making narrow but stout edgings for corsets and other underwear in the 1860s. In the twentieth century it turned to laces, with imitations of torchon and cluny, used for furnishing rather than fashion, though swimsuits were sometimes enlivened with narrow stripes. A further step in its development occurred in the 1970s with the ethnic fashion which demanded simple, bold and colourful peasant laces. These the Barmen could produce admirably in cotton, wool, jute or synthetics.

The Raschel was a post-war development using the warp-knitting principle of the old Warp Frame machine invented in the 1780s. From the 1840s its productions had failed to compete commercially with the twist net machines (Bobbinet, Leavers, Pusher) and it had turned to the making of non-lacy cloth fabrics. Now, with the ponderous Leavers suffering from escalating costs and a shortage of skilled labour, the Pusher defunct, and the Bobbinet almost unable to pattern, the Raschel turned back to the making of openworks. A tremendous impetus to this trend was provided by the development of synthetic fibres, since the machine's extremely rapid working placed a great strain on natural cottons, causing the needles to become repeatedly clogged with fluff. The synthetics, with their endlessly long filaments and their greater strength, did not do this (fig. 108).

However, despite its promising potential, the Raschel's laces had to wait on fashion, a wait which

112 *(a) A personalized lace design for Cocoa of Cheltenham. The clear yet unobtrusive name forms a pleasing pattern. By Roger Watson of Nottingham, 1983.*

(b) Four designs made on the Leavers machine, 1982.

lasted until the end of the 1960s. Then, a period of relative prosperity fostered an interest in solid investments which could hedge against inflation by their value rising more rapidly than that of the cost of living. Many artefacts, including old lace and antique dresses, became wanted and therefore sale-able for the first time in 40 years. As they flooded the market, young fashion designers seized them eagerly, and in no time at all were converting them into ranges of dreamy-looking froth and flounce which could still be sold at a mere fraction of the value of those laces 100 or more years before (fig. 109). Their ingenuity was endless: hand-made lace motifs were stitched to jeans and sweaters, berthas

113 *A flamboyant jacket made of a mass of edgings. The multiple tiers give it tremendous impact value, so that the effect of a lacy appearance, of lace draped all over the place (just as Louis XIV and all the royal Courts of Europe had centuries ago) is achieved here in the best way it can be, in today's world. By Caroline Charles of Knightsbridge, 1983.*

were tied around necks like scarves, Maltese stoles appeared as glowing turbans, fichus were cut up into enchanting Juliet caps, frilly Victorian night-dresses worn as summer skirts, and sleeveless white chemises as miniskirts.

Such a development was a two-edged sword – it brought lace back into fashion, but it also destroyed it. What obviously was required, if the fashion was to continue, were new laces which, having been used, could be replaced. For hand laces there could be no commercial revival except in low paid areas of the Far East, and even then the work, to be economic, had to be either coarse or simple or both so that although a great deal came to the European market, and was very competently made, it lacked the elegance and aplomb which would make it fashion.

Hand lace-making can never be speeded: it can only be badly paid. A four-inch wide Bucks point edging might take eight hours to make an inch. An example worked at the Great Exhibition of 1851, in finer thread (20-slip cotton) took three months to produce one foot (Channer). The needle lace point Colbert made at Bayeux in 1867–8 took one year to complete one metre which was then sold for 500 francs; while a garniture of point de gaze 'with raised flowers in floating relief', shown at the Vienna Exhibition of 1873 and consisting of a triangular shawl, a bertha, a parasol cover, fan, handkerchief, two seven-yard flounces and one six-yard 'took 12 of the most expensive lace makers 3 years to complete' and cost 40,000 francs (*The Queen Lace Book*) (fig. 110). Such consumption of time, and such prices, updated, are simply not economic in the last quarter of the twentieth century.

Machines on the other hand can go fast, and have always the possibility of further acceleration. The Raschel can knit nearly 12 inches of 130-inch wide fabric every minute. The Leavers can produce between one and three yards in length per hour, depending on quality, the higher qualities being slower to make. The Schiffli embroidery machine, so closely connected with fashion at the turn of the century, could also sponsor a return of lace to fashion, aided by the Bobbinet machine, which still turns out round-mesh nets in silk, nylon or cotton on precisely the same principle as that invented by Heathcoat in 1808–9, though the Brussels or diamond nets ceased production in the 1930s. The Schiffli's speed is timed not by tape measures but by the number of stitches, since its process is embroidery and the speed of completion of any piece must depend on the size and complexity of the design, in effect on the number of stitches required to make it. Larger machines work at about 150 to 200 stitches a minute; new and smaller machines are faster. Its embroideries on bobbinet can be sold as yardages sewn with bright gardens of flowers over coloured nylon.

The design of the Carrickmacross enlivening the bodice and sleeves of the Princess of Wales' wedding dress in 1981 was copied by the Schiffli machine to provide a sufficient length to border the train and skirt (fig. 111). The Schiffli also still produces chemical laces, though these are now embroidered on a backing of acetate rayon subsequently dissolved in acetone.

Thus machines hold the key to the future of lace in fashion. Given the consumers, they can produce the goods. The more demand increases, the more complex and beautiful will be the designs which it is economic for them to make (fig. 112). While hand lace-making is perpetuated as an art, so preserving for posterity the ingenious techniques of the old laces, machine products are ideal for dissemination in a busy and much travelled society (fig. 113). Unlike the laces of the past which needed extreme care, today's laces are for the most part tough, washable, relatively inexpensive and replaceable. With this practical aspect of its wearing in mind, there is no reason why lace, after a long and unproductive slumber, should not re-establish itself, or why the end of the twentieth century should not see a strong revival of lace in fashion, even though it is no longer fashion as originally defined.

6

Lace for Children
FASHION IN MINIATURE

The immature portion of a human life can be considered in three stages: babyhood, infancy, and childhood proper. The time needed to be spent in each stage must vary with the individual, but the time actually spent is more likely to be determined by social conventions, hand-in-glove with parental convenience.

It was social convention which decreed that children's fashions, from the sixteenth century to the second half of the eighteenth, were to be the fashions, in miniature, of their mothers and fathers. In no way were they adapted to the child's special needs, or preferences, partly because it is the fate of adults not to remember from their own experience what those needs and preferences were. Not until the eighteenth century did reformers try to look at things from a child's point of view, and not until the mid-nineteenth century did medical understanding begin to spell out the essentials for full mental and physical development.

Just as clothes were near-identical for children and parents up to this point of enlightenment, so too were the laces which decorated them. In this chapter, therefore, the aim will be to concentrate mainly on those shapes and types of lace which differed between adults and offspring, such as its use to decorate swaddling.

Babyhood: up to one year old

Swaddling
Though this practice appears more appropriate to a nomadic style of life where young babies have to be carried about on their mothers' backs, and must, while there, be prevented from crumpling into a disorganized heap, nevertheless it does appear to have been universally practised in settled European communities over hundreds of years. Basically it consisted of binding the baby in linen or woollen bands criss-crossed mummy-like around it, leaving only the head free, and even that supported by a series of stay-tapes so that it could not wobble too far in any direction. Various alternative swaddling procedures were used, but all had the same effect, the prohibition of movement, and the enforced straightening of the limbs. For royal and aristocratic offspring the swaddling bands might be edged with a punto in aria lace or, later, a Flemish bobbin such as their parents wore (fig. 114). Their tiny ruffs, their biggins (close-fitting caps), and their muckinders (squares of linen used to wipe slobber from the face and nose), all of which appear in church effigies of the late sixteenth and early seventeenth centuries, were similarly decorated. Arms were freed from swaddling after the first few months, but legs were bound for up to a year, except for the not infrequent unwrappings to remove dirtied 'tail-clouts'.

The reform of this frustrating imprisonment appears to have started in England. John Locke's *Thoughts on Education*, published in 1693, found a receptive audience. The less suave and diplomatic attacks on the very foundations of eighteenth-century society by Jean-Jacques Rousseau in *Emile ou de l'Education*, 1762, aroused a storm of counter-attacks by governments, who burnt his books, and a storm of alarm in the breast of Mrs Delany who, hearing that he was intending to settle at Wotton, felt obliged to warn her niece Mary against his possible evil influence.

By 1769 swaddling was ridiculed in England: 'those rollers and wrappers applied to the baby's body as if every bone had been fractured at birth', and 'the barbarous custom of swaddling children like living mummies, is now almost universally laid aside' (1785).[1] The rigid formalities of the French Court were, however, offended when, in 1778, Marie Antoinette refused to swaddle her first-born, Madame Royale. Swaddling continued well into the nineteenth century in European peasant communities (see figs 115, 150).

Shirts
In the sixteenth and seventeenth centuries these were worn under the swaddling bands, and were fairly short so that they were not too chronically wet. The necks fitted round the base of the throat,

114 *The future Louis XIV with his first nurse, Marie Longuet de la Giraudière. His cap, collar, shirt and swaddling bands are all trimmed with Flemish bobbin lace. Attributed to Charles Beaubrun, 1638–9.*

the front was open, and the sleeves long, ending in tiny cuffs fastened by links. The neck, shoulder seams and sleeve ends were decorated with lace. Laces of black silk and gold metal are recorded, probably from the north Italian centres of Genoa, Lucca and Milan; also fine linen laces from Flanders. Handsome christening shirts were a traditional gift from the godparents, and their lace alone might cost a noble (10s, or in present-day equivalence not less than £20).

During the eighteenth century, godparents gave not shirts alone but christening sets which included, in addition, a decorated outer cap, a plain undercap, a long bib, a forehead piece, and a pair of cuffs. In England these were traditionally decorated with the needle lace hollie point (fig. 116).

In the nineteenth century a similar type of shirt continued to be worn, protecting the baby's skin from the irritation of the flannel binder which still encompassed its middle. It was now, however, covered by a gown of some kind, so that it had more the function of an undergarment or vest, and was simpler. Its neck was wide, its sleeves little more than epaulettes, and the lace when present both narrow and very plain, such as Bucks or Lille or, after about 1850, knitted lace, crochet, tatting, torchon, or Barmen machine braid. In the twentieth century, openwork knitting on baby vests was their only claim to laciness.

Caps and bonnets

Baby caps appear always to have been close-fitting and shaped to follow the curves of the head. Not until infancy did caps begin to copy the grown-up form (fig. 117).

In the early seventeenth century scalloped Flemish collar laces were used for trimmings; later, the finer Binche, Mechlin and Valenciennes. In the eighteenth century hollie point was used in England. In the nineteenth century caps had dainty hand-sprigging in white embroidery of a type known as Ayrshire work, which combined surface embroidery with drawn threadwork, or the use of needle lace stitches (fig. 118). By the 1830s caps were

trimmed more elaborately with muslin frills, or with several rows of narrowly pretty Lille or Northants laces. Sometimes they were made of insertions of Mechlin lace stitched together, or of plain lawn with cap crowns of Bucks point. This latter innovation, started by James Millward in the 1840s, enjoyed a great success, especially in exports to the former American colonies, until trade in that direction was ended by the American Civil War of 1861–5 (fig. 119).

A plainer undercap was commonly worn beneath the outer decorative one. It was kept on both night and day until, in 1856, the medical profession announced its opinion that 'the head is much better kept at as low a temperature as the room ought to be where the baby is', and suggested that to achieve this end the head should be left bare. That the advice was followed is indicated by a comment in *The Englishwoman's Domestic Magazine* of 1868 where it is recommended that squares of flannel be constantly available to throw over a baby's head as it was carried from one room to another.

Veils of net had long been used to cover the baby's face outdoors, just as they had for women, to protect their skins from the sun. An earlier form, described in 1575, was of 'lawne striped with bone lace of gold'.[2] The somewhat fanatical Dr Jaeger, in the 1860s, instituted veils of lacy-knitted wool. Twenty years later wool was condemned as unfit for this purpose.

For babies and children, as for adults, the nineteenth century, which began with a near absence of lace, ended in a cascading surfeit. Babies' bonnets, tied on with ribbons, became submerged in a superabundance of heavy Swiss guipures, Irish crochets, and the products of the Swiss hand embroidery machines (fig. 120).

Christening mantles/bearing cloths

In the sixteenth century these were square or rectangular cloths of silk or velvet, bordered with gold and silver laces and decorated with sequins. The baby was wrapped in one end and carried by its nurse, while the long empty end was supported by noble attendants.

Such mantles continued in use in the seventeenth and early eighteenth centuries. In 1623 one is described as being trimmed with 11 ounces of lace, costing 57s (£2.85), which is quite a weight, indicating that a precious metal such as gold was probably used. The mantle for the christening of Louis XIV's grandson (1682) and his great-grandson (1707) took the form of deep flounces of point de France around the cushion on which the child was carried (fig. 121).

115 *Marie Antoinette with her three children: Madame Royale, the Dauphin (died 1789) and the future Louis XVII (died 1793, aged nine). The Queen wears Alençon lace on her bodice, sleeves and large feathered hat; her daughter has a lace tucker and cuffs; the Dauphin wears a lace collar over his jacket, and a sash around his trousers; the baby a white gown and a lace cap, all Alençon. By Vigée Lebrun, 1786.*

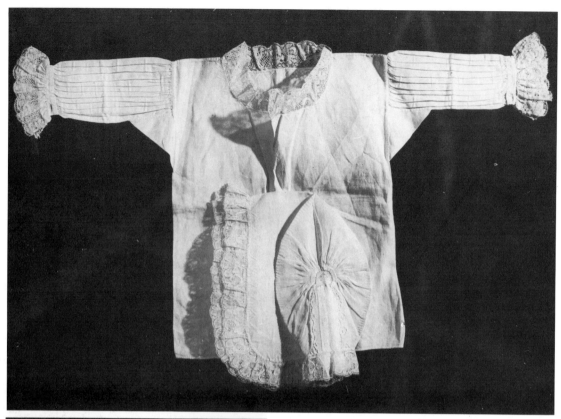

116 *Part of a christening set, early eighteenth century. The back of the cap and the shoulders of the shirt are inset with hollie point, and trimmed with bobbin lace.*

117 *A baby cap decorated with cutwork of reticella type. The bands are edged with a stout bobbin lace, possibly Scandinavian, early seventeenth century.*

In the later eighteenth century the christening mantle became more like a gown, a fitted garment of ivory satin, shaped like a woman's sacque, with the skirt opened to disclose a quilted petticoat. It was usually decorated not with lace but with tasselled braid and fringing, sometimes in pale shades of pink and blue.

By the nineteenth century babies were being carried in shawls of white hand-woven cashmere, or of wool or silk knitted lace. In the 1830s and '40s these knitted lace shawls achieved a great fineness, and were sometimes known as zephyrs. Lacy Shetland shawls also became popular for babies at this time.

Christening gowns
These were white dresses of lawn, muslin or net, which were a good deal longer than the baby, and a good deal fancier than ordinary day-gowns. They

118 *A baby bonnet with Ayrshire-work crown. The mother wears a white embroidered apron, cap and fichu. 'Hickory, Dickory Dock' by Edith Hipkins, c.1840.*

119 *(top right) A cap back of Bucks point, as made by James Millward, 1840–60.*

120 *The elaborate baby bonnets and mantles of the 1890s. The Queen, 1897.*

(a)

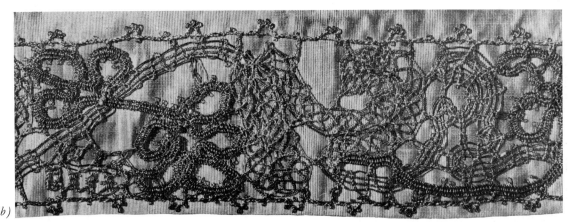

(b)

121 *(a) The newly-born Duke of Burgundy, son of Monseigneur (the Grand Dauphin), is presented to his grandfather, King Louis XIV, in 1682. Over his swaddled body hangs a bearing cloth flounced with point de France. The men wear justaucorps with lace cravats and ruffled shirt sleeves below. The women have lace berthas, ruffles and flounces but, except for the mother still in bed, and the two servants (the nurse, and Madame la Motte who holds the baby) they are bare-headed. In a similar engraving, of the Duke of Burgundy's second son, in 1707, the ladies wear commodes.*

(b) Detail of the gimp lace border, in gold and silver thread, of a bearing cloth of the early eighteenth century.

were a late eighteenth-century innovation, and followed the rising and falling waistline, the simplicity or over-elaboration, the V-shaped bodice or the princess line of adult fashion, but not its extreme vicissitudes of nipped-in waists, crinolines, bloated sleeves and bustles, which were all reserved for the next phase, of infancy.

All nineteenth-century christening gowns, except for the earliest, plainest ones, had lace, though it varied considerably in quality and quantity. All, until the end of the century, had low necklines and short sleeves. The following are four of their typical decorations:

(a) *Ayrshire*, c.1814–70. Though mainly a form of embroidery it included openwork areas filled with drawnwork, or needle lace, or with plain or decorated nets. From its perennially floral designs the work was called flowerin', especially in Ireland, and the makers, flowerers (fig. 122). In the twentieth century, coarser copies with less openwork were made in India, and also by the Moravian sisters of Fairfield, near Manchester.

(b) *Appliqué work*, late eighteenth century to the present day. Hand-made bobbin or needle lace motifs were stitched to a machine net or, mostly

before 1815, to a hand-made droschel. The technique was favoured by Honiton laces in England, and Brussels in Belgium. Examples are the gown first made for Victoria's second child, the Prince of Wales, in 1841; and for the future Queen Wilhelmina in 1880 (fig. 123). Woven cottons were also appliquéd to machine nets either by chain stitch, or by a couched outlining cord, as in Carrickmacross.

(c) *Broderie anglaise/Madeira work*, c.1850–80. This was in essence a revival of early sixteenth-century cutworks. Holes, either circular or pear-shaped, were made with a stiletto, a punch, or scissors, and

122 *An Ayrshire gown, c.1840.*

123 *(a) The Royal Christening Gown of Honiton appliqué on net, first worn by Albert Edward, Prince of Wales, in 1841.*
(b) Detail.
(c) The Brussels appliqué christening gown of Queen Wilhelmina of the Netherlands, 1880.

embroidered around to prevent fraying.

(d) *Swiss embroidered machine laces*, 1860–1910, made on the hand machine. These could be bought by the yard as edging or insertion. They were often used to alternate with bands of a simply designed hand lace such as Valenciennes or Bucks point. It was a style which particularly suited the princess line, introduced around 1870. For babies, the illusion of a waistline was created on their barrel-like forms by a tapered-in bodice continuous with a swelling skirt, which did not decrease the size of the waist, but appeared to do so. Down the whole centre panel swept cascades of tucks and trimming. Skirts were lengthened to accommodate yet more, reaching a total of some 45 inches (fig. 124).

A few more years and baby dresses became simple, short and practical, and from the 1920s lace had no serious or consistent place in fashion for babies, infants or children. However a favoured few, offspring of lace-making mothers or grandmothers, were the fortunate wearers of delectable gowns trimmed with narrow Bucks point, Beds or torchon, all beautifully made. They were not, however, worn consistently by a whole group of people, and so were not fashion as strictly defined, just as the fine heirloom baby gowns of the aristocracy lacked that other prerequisite of fashion, its fickleness.

124 *(a) (above) The elegant impracticability of the mother's house gown is mirrored in the elaborate ribbon and lace frills worn by her baby, 1873.*
(b) (below) Narrow nylon laces for babies in 1958.

125 *An expensive layette with pillows, basinette and baby gown all trimmed with luxurious lace, and the coverlet entirely of blonde. Thought to be the Infanta Dona Carlotta Joaquinna de Bourbon, by Anton Raphael Mengs, 1770s.*

Noble layettes were likely to cost a lot of money. The baby garments and cradle trappings of the Duke of Reichstadt, son of Napoleon I, born in 1811, were all of Alençon spangled with Ns, crowns and stars. That of a future marquis in 1821 cost £2,000, and included many laces from Brussels. That of the Prince Imperial, son of Napoleon III and the Empress Eugénie cost, in 1856, £60,000. It included a christening robe at £1,000, scores of tiny lace-trimmed gowns, mantles and pelisses, and a cradle decked in white velvet overlaid with Alençon (*Illustrated London News*). (See fig. 125.)

Infancy: one to seven years

This intermediate period of development was variable in length according to the custom of the times. Five to seven years was usual in the sixteenth century, four or five years in the seventeenth, and six years in the eighteenth and nineteenth centuries. Initially, and until the mid-eighteenth century, infancy began with a switch from baby clothes to

126 *Henry Prince of Wales, eldest son of James I, in elaborate coif, collar, cuffs and gown, all decorated with finely wrought punto in aria. A miniature, School of Isaac Oliver, 1595.*

127 *All three children wear elaborate clothes, the boy and elder girl with a suggestion of a farthingale. Their varying collar shapes, and upright cuffs, are edged with bobbin lace imitating punto in aria. All three have broad shoe roses, and their sashes are deeply fringed with gold lace. The boy wears a doublet, not a bodice, with his skirt, and he carries a sword. The youngest child's go-cart stands at the side, while her sister holds her leading strings. The painting is dated 161–, entitled 'James the I Familey', and the ages of the children given as 5, 2, 4. The dates of birth of James's three eldest – Henry, Elizabeth and Margaret, born in 1594, 1596 and 1598 respectively – make 1600 or 1601 a likely year for the painting. Robert Peake.*

the tight discomfort of miniature female fashion. Boys, like girls, wore petticoats or 'coats'. This advancement was called 'shortening' or 'short-coating', indicating that the gowns, though adult in form, were reduced in length so that impetuous feet were not too hazardously cluttered. Boys sometimes wore lace-trimmed coifs, like their sisters, though they discarded them more quickly (figs 126, 127, 128).

With the era of enlightenment in the mid-eighteenth century, babyhood was allowed to encroach a little on infancy, and a small girl's second birthday might be attained before her ribs were crushed by constricting stays and her skirts elevated by a hoop. By the 1760s and '70s, babyish white dresses, tied with a blue sash, were being worn by three- and then four-year-olds, to be followed by modifications still not quite as demanding as adult styles. Lace-trimmed shifts were exposed at the neck and elbows. The paintings of Arthur Devis (1711–87) show infants with filmy fichus crossed at the waist, translucent muslin aprons, tiered cobwebs of engageants below ruched cuffs ascending the upper arms, delicate narrow frills at the neckline, and small round-eared caps also narrowly frilled. Adults in his portraits might sit awkwardly on their newly-acquired estates as if, having at last got in, they were afraid of being found out; but the doll-like children had no such qualms.

Infant boys were freed at last from caps and corsets, and from the age of about three were put into white satin suits with sleeved jackets, and trousers extending to about mid-calf. By the 1770s the trousers reached down to the ankles, and might be full or tight-fitting, in which latter case they were known as pantaloons. A sash was tied at the junction between shirt and trouser top. Shirts were open at the neck, and the collar was spread over the jacket with a frilled edging of muslin or a narrow lace (see fig. 115).

For girls, soft muslin dresses continued to be worn for longer and longer periods until they filled the whole era of infancy, and began to extend beyond. Bare shoulders emerged above plain short-sleeved bodices, and were covered by muslin handkerchiefs crossed at the front and tied in a bow behind. Mob caps, graced with a ribbon bow, bulged balloon-like over their foreheads, and lace was entirely, or almost, absent.

By the end of the eighteenth century even adults had adopted this infant style, and for a brief halcyon period children rejoiced in comfort. The trousers of young boys now fastened with big buttons over a jacket. The whole fitted closely to the body, and was known as a 'skeleton suit', a style which remained

popular for the next 40 years, until the onset of Victorianism and a renewed triumph of adult vanity over infantile ease (fig. 129).

For most of the nineteenth century, the time during which boys were dressed like girls remained at three years. In this period of early infancy both wore, beneath calf-length dresses, long white drawers edged with lace. These sometimes came down from the waist, but were sometimes 'shams',

128 *Infant laces of the seventeenth century:*

(a) A lawn apron seamed and edged with needle lace, the bib overlaid with a flat collar beneath a gollila, the lace of the coif forming a starry tiara. By Cornelius de Vos, c.1620.

(b) A young infant squashed into a stiffened bodice. The rabat-style collar, cuffs and bibbed apron are all bordered with a finely-textured Antwerp bobbin lace. Dutch school, c.1660.

(c) Louis XIV with his younger brother the Duke of Orléans (born 1640) in 'coats', with coifs, aprons and falling collars of intricate Flemish bobbin laces. By Charles Beaubrun.

that is short tubes tied with tapes above the knee so that they did nothing except provide the requisite visual impression (fig. 130).

Dresses and drawers became shorter in the mid-century, and drawers ultimately disappeared beneath the skirt. Broderie anglaise was used a lot, on central panels of the bodice and skirt, and as trimmings which gave an open-robe effect in keeping with the imitation of eighteenth-century styles favoured by adult females (colour plate 4). Bare shoulders could be covered with matching capes and tippets, or by sleeved jackets known as pardessus. Dresses for the under-threes were, more

than anything, like chopped-off versions of their christening gowns.

Once the third birthday was passed, infancy might as well have been over. Fashions for small girls regressed to uncomfortable, even cruel, versions of their mothers' clothes (fig. 131). Boys gave up dresses, and also the skeleton suit which by the 1840s was out of fashion, and went into a tunic, not unlike a man's frock coat but knee-length, belted at the waist, and sometimes having outside it a lace collar. Beneath the tunic appeared, incongruously, cotton drawers worn over thick stockings encased in boots.

In the 1860s boys' drawers were transformed into knee breeches, and a really masculine knickerbocker suit made its appearance. This lasted until the 1880s when an extraordinary version of it, known as the Fauntleroy suit, emerged in America. It was described in *The Lady* as 'a tunic and knickerbockers of sapphire blue velvet, a sash of pale pink, and a Vandyke collar and cuffs, if not of old point lace then of Irish guipure.' 'Old point' was simply the popular name for the post-1850s tape or renaissance lace which aimed to copy antique styles. 'Irish guipure' referred to Irish crochet with its heavy flowers and wide picoted meshes.

For some time after 1900 only babies wore unisex clothes, and boy and girl infants, once they were fully mobile, were discriminated by their garments. Neither had much use for lace. Dresses made of openwork knitting, or trimmed with Barmen-type braids, were almost the only decorations favoured by an increasingly utilitarian society, though children of the rich might continue to boast of their Brussels-trimmed frocks, or the Valenciennes lace on their knickers.

After the Second World War, infants were once more dressed alike, only now it was small girls who wore T-shirts and trousers, in imitation of small boys. There was still no use for lace until, along with the appearance of old lace on the market in the late 1960s, hoards of white infant dresses from Victorian and Edwardian times became available. But the fashion was ephemeral. They were quite impractical for daily wear, and quickly disintegrated in the washing machine.

Childhood: over seven

In the sixteenth and seventeenth centuries, clothes for the over-sevens were no more and no less than adult costume on a smaller scale, with only the most minimal concessions to the need for comfort and growth. Girls had already been wearing grown-up styles in infancy, so that no significant change was involved. For boys the change was more drastic: they were 'breeched', and progressed from long skirts to doublet and hose or, later, doublet and breeches. There was usually a brief interlude when, instead of a feminine bodice, young boys wore a masculine doublet, with a sword belt, over the skirt (see fig. 127). The scarf from which the sword hung was sometimes trimmed with a gold lace of dentate form. The sequence of laces through the years followed faithfully those worn by men, and as men gradually discarded lace, so did male children (fig. 132).

Girls, mirroring in childhood, as they had in infancy, their mothers' laces, wore aprons, handkerchiefs, coifs, ruffs and collars. Their chests confined to leather 'bodies', their skirts extended by hoops or farthingales, they suffered just as did their mothers 'to attain a wand-like smalnesse of waste' though it was already recognized that this could lead to 'consumptions' and a 'withering rottennesse'.[3]

129 *The Duke of Reichstad, King of Rome, son of Napoleon I, wearing a skeleton suit, with a frilled collar of Alençon needle lace. By Carl von Sales, c.1815.*

130 *Two children in dresses and drawers. The lace on the girl's drawers, similar to a Northants bobbin lace, may have been made in New England. The boy has no lace. By Jefferson Gaunt, c.1830.*

(a)

(b)

(c)

131 (a) An infant's dress in white cambric, the front en tablier (shaped like an apron) with bands and robings of broderie anglaise.

(b) A girl's dress with tightened waist and crinoline skirt, with broderie anglaise in layered frills. The sleeves are secured by elastic bands, and are removable (see colour plate 4). Both 1850s, Godey's Ladies' Book.

(c) The adult style for young girls, 1874.

The lace-trimmed caps and coifs of infancy were sometimes exchanged for more mature accessories as girls neared their teens. In the late seventeenth century a fontange might be worn even by young girls, though in England it was restricted to the royal family (fig. 133). In the eighteenth century lace-trimmed caps were perched on top of the head, or joined beneath the chin. Lacy gloves or mittens of sprang, filet or warp lace were customary, and so were fans, though these were rarely of lace.

In the 1820s there was a brief flutter into Turkish trousers, an innovation viewed with horror by the

132 *The young boy wears an adult-style rabat, lace cuffs and canons, along with a hat, short doublet, billowy shirt, petticoat breeches trimmed with rows of ribbons, and wide shoe strings. Thomas de Keyser, c.1660.*

133 *The Princess Louise, daughter of James II and Mary of Modena his second wife, aged three, and dressed like an adult of the period. Her tall fontange with the lappets pinned up, her stomacher, cuffs and apron are all of point de France. Nicholas de Largillière, 1695, detail.*

moralists who, keen on maintaining the image of the submissive woman, condemned this prospect of girlish masculinization. Thereafter not until the 1890s did comfort return for adolescents. Then a loose smock, falling from a yoke and caught to a low waist with a belt, was brought in, a style which had no exact counterpart in the adult world.

Throughout the nineteenth century female infants and children wore protective pinafores over their dresses. These were a practical replacement for the decorative aprons worn in earlier centuries, and marked, perhaps, a recognition that children should be allowed to get dirty. Pinafores were of strong materials, and were at first essentially plain, with a narrow border of openwork embroidery, crochet,

or some other stout and resilient lace. In the 1890s they became more fancy, with yokes of lace projecting over the arms in starched palisades. Bonnets worn out of doors were smothered in ribbon rosettes nestling in lacy frills. Openwork knitting on socks and stockings constituted also a form of lace in fashion.

The twentieth century elevated the production of children's clothes to the status of big business. Psychology had established the child as already in its tenderest years an individual in its own right, needing clothes suited to its specific non-adult requirements, and doubtless in time deciding, for itself, whether lace had any part to play in the fashions it favoured.

7
Lace on Underwear
THE FOUNDATIONS OF FASHION

Underwear relates, by its very name, to hidden garments, worn under garments which are displayed. Yet the origin of the linen laces of fashion – as opposed to those of silver and gold which were intended from the first to be flaunted – was on undergarments, just at those points where they protruded beyond the overgarments which it was their function to protect. Here, where undergarments were visible, they cried out for decoration, and the obvious choice was an openwork embroidery similar to that which had already for some time been used on household and ecclesiastical linen.

In this way the primary function of underwear, that of preventing the heat and moisture of the body from staining or otherwise damaging the expensive and difficult-to-clean overgarments, became at an early stage linked with the secondary function of providing visible embellishment.

The third function of underwear, that of changing the human shape by exaggeration or diminution of the bust, waist or hips, and a fourth tardily developed function of keeping the wearer warm, had nothing to do with lace in fashion, and will not be referred to in this chapter, except in the most incidental manner.

The sixteenth century

The development of lace in fashion, described in Chapter 1, is in effect the story of lace on underwear up to the point where the embroidered lace extensions of those linen garments became so complex and so difficult to wash that they had to be constructed as separate appendages (see figs 7, 13).

It was mainly the garment known as the shirt for men, and the smock, shift or chemise for women, which was involved in this development, and what is said below applies equally to both.

Where the shirt neck was round, it began to rise up towards the throat, turning outwards at the top in a little frill. This frill, at first plain, was then edged with purling, or semi-circular loops of gold thread, built up into shallow triangles along its border.

When the out-turned frills became magnified into large millstones – extending nine inches or more outwards from the neck, decorated all over with cutwork, and with lace teeth bared along every flute – then ruffs became overwear, and any connection with underwear was completely severed.

Where the shirt neck had a small collar turned down over a high-necked doublet, it was given on a small scale the same cutwork and dentate edgings which characterized the ruff. Growing larger, and separating, such a collar became either a tiered falling ruff, sometimes with disorganized fluting (called a confusion ruff), or a cape-like falling collar made either entirely of lace or of two or three layers of linen each bordered with lace, until finally for women the whole thing narrowed and slipped downwards as a bertha encircling bare shoulders.

Where the shirt neck was open, and V-shaped, the exposed revers, embroidered in openwork on the reverse side, rose eventually behind the head in a standing, or Medici, collar pierced with cutwork and supported sometimes against a curved screen of gauze. Standing ruffs of several fluted layers were variations of this theme, as were the more horizontal or slightly tilted open ruffs, like millstones with a gap at the front.

In the sixteenth century skirts were sometimes opened to expose the petticoat, which was thus a semi-undergarment. However it was seldom, at this time, trimmed with lace.

The seventeenth century

In the seventeenth century what was worn beneath, yet alone whether it had lace on it or not, is still obscure. However the petticoat, exposed between the parted sides of the overskirt, soon became an area for display, and the classic example of Lady Castlemain's petticoat 'laced with rich lace that ever I saw' has been discussed (page 51). In 1660 Pepys had, grudgingly, parted with £5 (not less than £200 today) to buy silver lace for his wife's petticoat, though it vexed him later that it showed up so little against her pale grey silk.

Lace, whether of thread, silver, or merely printed, continued to be worn on petticoats for at least the next 40 years. It was often in deep flounces, such as the quilted petticoat 'with broad Flanders lace below' described by John Evelyn's daughter Mary, in a verse published in 1690. The Flanders lace would be of the luxurious form referred to in contemporary French engravings as point d'Angleterre. Flounces might also be of the needle lace point de France, shown in paintings of the second half of the century, and referred to in documents.

Stockings in the seventeenth century showed the same double aspect of over- and under-wear, being exposed for men and concealed for women. Their only connection with lace was in the boot hose, which were coarse linings to boots of Spanish leather, intended to protect the expensive silk stockings from friction. The flaring boot tops were filled with a froth of lace which spilled out from them like a vase overflowing with white flowers. Such laces, acting as decorations to the lower leg, were sometimes known as canions, though in general this term was used for the lace frills attached to the lower end of the breeches, either above or below the knee, where they were indisputably overwear.

With the eradication of the more protuberant neck and wrist pieces – such as ruffs, Medici collars, and their corresponding cuffs – from fashion during the 1620s, an era of softer styles began. Embroidered laces, worked in the actual fabric of the linen underwear, were no longer in fashion, and so of necessity the lace trim of shirts or shifts had to be bobbin or needle laces, made quite separately, even if they were later stitched on around the neck, down the front opening, or at the sleeve ends. Underwear was thus once again carrying lace which would enhance the overwear, though not now as an integral part of itself; and the large falling collars, and the later masculine rabats and cravats, were all quite separate. For women the shifts were trimmed, from the time when the falling collar became outdated, with a tucker which poked out above the stomacher of the formal dress. In informal 'undress' the tucker extended entirely round the smock's wide neckline, which might fall off the shoulders leaving most of the upper body bare. Lace ruffles trimmed the smock's sleeve ends, which might be short, or elbow-length.

Though the mode of wearing the lace, and the extent of its connection with underwear varied between men and women, the type of lace itself was similar, with needle laces being the more formally fashionable. Of these the most splendid were the Venetian gros points with their large sculptured flowers. Point de France was also used for the tuckers and ruffles attached to chemises, as well as for petticoats.

Nightwear, which might also be called underwear, being for the most part hidden beneath bedclothes, is revealed in seventeenth-century paintings (fig. 134) as exactly similar to that worn during the day as a smock or shirt, if not indeed the identical garment.

As for drawers, only those used as linings to petticoat breeches, in the second half of the seventeenth century, were at all visible. Emerging from the open ends of the overgarments, they were caught into a band around the knee by garters which sprouted lace frills, or which had canions attached. The broad legs of the breeches themselves were sometimes weighted with gold fringe to prevent their being lifted by the wind.

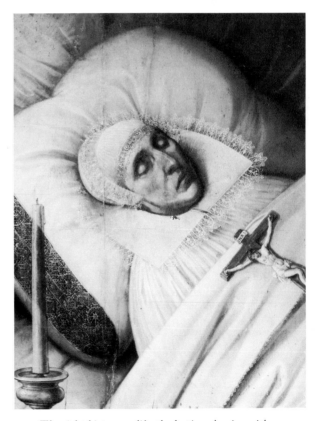

134 *The nightshirt worn, like the daytime chemise, with a standing collar of gollila type edged with a fine punto in aria which carries a design of vases of flowers, and matches that of the coif, worn over a nightcap. The pillow is seamed with a broad reticella. 'A Lady on her Deathbed', English School, 1626.*

135 *The Court mantua has a blue satin petticoat supported by a middle-sized panier and lavishly banded with Argentan lace and tails of marten fur held by white ribbon bows. By Voysard after Le Clerc, c.1770.*

The eighteenth century

'The first part of my dress,' said Lady Mary Wortley Montague in 1717, 'is a pair of drawers, very full, that reach to my shoes.'[1] She does not say whether they had lace. Although linen, or 'Holland', drawers, male and female, are referred to from the 1560s, lace in connection with them is not mentioned even in the eighteenth century.

Eighteenth-century petticoats, exposed by the open skirts of the sacque, or of the close-bodied gowns, sometimes had swags of lace looping across them but also, at least as commonly, tassels, fringing, jewels and embroidery. On the Court mantuas, cut from silk patterned with an extraordinary richness, only the glitter of equally rich precious-metal laces, applied lavishly in broad swathes, stood any chance at all of being observed (fig. 135).

Shifts, until the 1760s or '70s, were still the garments to which tuckers and engageants were attached, for laces were easier to remove from the linen, and to replace again after washing, than if stitches had actually to penetrate the heavy silken fabrics of the gown. The removable laces were provided with a little extra footing, separately attached to them, and it was this additional piece which took the strain of the repeated stitching as well as the tug and pull of movements during wear. The form of the top-quality Flemish bobbin or French needle laces of this century has been described in Chapter 3; so has their changing appearance and texture from the mid-century on, when lightly patterned narrower bobbin laces such as Lille, Bucks and blonde, were worn for semi-formal occasions by anyone who had society pretensions.

An important development in stockings dates from the late 1760s. Triggered by a minimal raising of the hemline of women's gowns so that the ankles were exposed, fashion lost no time in drawing attention to this new area of view by means of decorative openworks above the instep. Such openworks could be made by three techniques: openwork hand-knitting using fine silk thread and extremely thin needles; separation of the stitches of plain-knitted hose by a form of embroidery so that openwork patterns were formed; and manipulation by hand of the stitch-loops on the Stocking Frame machine, using the tip of a thin wire known as a tickler.

Nightwear, as in the later seventeenth century, referred exclusively to the wear of the night, while 'nightgown' meant instead a casual form of overwear, or undress. Nightwear was virtually the same thing as daytime shirts or chemises, while nightgowns were additional garments worn over them, in just the same way as was more formal attire. Cravats for men, and tippets for women, whether of lace or not, were separate pieces.

The nineteenth century

Infinitely more information is available about underwear, and the lace on it, in the nineteenth century. Indeed, few secrets remain, while many actual garments survive to make sense of the written records. There are even inventories of the types and quantity of underwear a lady of moderately ample means – say £2,000 a year in 1873, equivalent to about £21,000 today – would be expected to amass for her trousseau. Part of the list reads: '3 dozen chemises, 3 doz drawers, 12 doz nightdresses, 12 doz hosiery, 1 doz flannel petticoats, 1 doz flannel vests, 3 doz white petticoats. . . .'[2]

The neo-classical style of the turn of the century brought about, little by little, a change in the nature of the chemise. It drew back, gradually, inside the gown so that visible laces were no longer attached to it, and in time it became no more that a short-sleeved sweat absorber clamped to the skin by the severe grip of the corset around it (fig. 136). Corsets had been cruelly tight almost continuously since fashion began. 'I hope Miss Sparrow will not fall into the absurd fashion of ye *wasp-waisted* ladies,' wrote Mrs Delany in 1780, 'Dr Pringle declares he has had four of his patients martyrs to that folly, and when they were opened it was evident that their *deaths* were occasioned by *strait lacing*.'[3]

The visibly decorative function lost by the chemise was taken over in the 1830s by the chemisette (Fig. 137). The lost lace ruffles, similarly, were replaced by undersleeves, sometimes called engageants. Both were only marginally underwear, the chemisette being exposed except where it ducked down beneath the bodice and was tied by tapes around the waist; while the undersleeves, their decoration taking the form of openwork embroidery which matched that of the chemisette, were hidden only where they disappeared within the open ends of the sleeves to be fixed about the elbow by a thin cord run through them. Tamboured net was also sometimes used, this like the white embroidery being an economic substitute for bobbin or needle laces, since it was quicker and easier to make, and therefore cheaper.

The chemisette of the 1840s–'60s became the vestee of the 1880s–'90s with a dog- or choker-collar attached to its upper part. It started inside the bodice and ended outside, and was only dubiously underwear. It was often made entirely of the bold guipure laces such as Irish crochet, Maltese or Bruges; or, like other accessories, of fine antique laces cut from old flounces. Plain or patterned machine nets might also be used. The closely related plastron, or breastplate, was similar to the vestee except that it lay entirely over the bodice, and was frequently used to conceal its opening.

A new undergarment, the camisole, appeared in the mid-nineteenth century. Its purpose was to cover the corset which was for the most part neither beautiful to look at nor particularly easy to clean. The camisole was waist-length, fitted smoothly, and might have cotton machine laces encircling the scooped neck and the short sleeves, or the wide shoulder straps. Alternatively, as with the chemise, the trimmings could be tatting or crochet, or narrow but durable bobbin laces such as torchon, which was also a post-1850s innovation (figs 138, 139). The peak of fashion lace for such garments

136 *The order of putting on: the lace-trimmed chemise and petticoat are covered by the laced corset. On the right, a fichu with lace and white embroidery. 1837.*

was fine quality Valenciennes, made at a number of centres in Belgium, or of coarser quality at Bailleul in France. A neatly subdued design was favoured by Queen Victoria, while the Empress Eugénie preferred a broader, more elaborately patterned form.

For men the eighteenth-century style of shirt continued for a short while, with lace ruffles and an occasional cravat. Both persisted longer for formal wear. But shirts were soon laceless and definitely overwear. Another new garment, the vest, now appeared beneath them – not to be confused with the vest worn over the shirt, which had now in England been renamed the waistcoat.

Dr Jaeger played some part in the development of the new vest. Under the influence of his fanatical cult of wool, this despised fibre – 'odious' in the eighteenth century, and unpopular even for burials in the seventeenth (page 45) – became the latest craze. The only connection with lace which these vests had was that, for women, Jaeger undergarments were sometimes of openwork knitting, or lacy-knits, made on the Stocking Frame, while in the 1890s they were being trimmed with a 'creamy

137 *Lingerie, late 1840s. The triangular chemisettes have 'Peter Pan' collars, the separate sleeves are shown beside them.*

138 *(a) Corsets from Paris with veritable ballein (real whalebone), laced at the back, threaded with ribbon, and trimmed with a narrow machine lace. Mid-nineteenth century.*

(b) The top of a sleeveless chemise, 1877. Below, a suggested decoration of point lace and white embroidery for the neckline.

wool lace'. This lace was probably 'yak', a torchon-style bobbin lace made of worsted in many areas including the East Midlands of England, and Le Puy in central France. Lace-makers found wool tricky to use, not only because the scales on the wool fibres caught against each other as the threads were tightened, so that it was difficult to make the work completely regular, but also because the weight of the bobbins stretched the wool. Then, when the pins were removed and the tension released, its elasticity caused it to spring back so that it shrank to some two-thirds of its original size.

Petticoats in the nineteenth century became entirely covered by skirts and thus, like the chemise, true undergarments. From that time they were not revealed to the public eye except by accident, at least until the 1870s when the passing of the crinoline and the reintroduction of dresses with a long train made

the raising of small areas of the skirt hem by a specially constructed skirt lifter a necessary precaution to avoid tripping over it. The quantity of lace on most garments had always been directly proportional to the extent to which it would be seen, and the same was true here. On the many stout petticoats of the 1850s' crinolines, broderie anglaise – also known as Madeira work or eyelet embroidery – formed a broad band along the hem, its bold openness the only effective decoration of fabric on such a massive scale.

In the suave lines of the 1870s and '80s, though the greater part of the lacy decoration lay on the skirts above, tiered like successive effusions of lava cascading over each other in gathers, pleats and eschelles, petticoats too became immensely more elegant. Where previously they had begun at the waist and extended to just above the hemline, now they were frequently united with the shaped top and narrow waist of the camisole to form the princess petticoat, named after Alexandra, Duchess of York, later Princess of Wales. Eyelet embroidery, delicately made on the Swiss hand machine, encircled the short sleeves and low neckline, while row upon row of starched and frilled machine laces, patterned like Valenciennes, held out the elaborate tail of the skirt as it literally swept the floor.

The exact form of the nineteenth-century drawers is revealed in literature, paintings, drawings and actual garments. The Princess Charlotte, aged 15, when accused of showing her drawers too blatantly as she sat with her legs sprawled out in front of her, retorted that the Duchess of Bedford's drawers were much longer *and* they were trimmed with Brussels lace.[4]

Drawers at first took the form of two tubes, one for each leg, with no junction between them except at the waist. Sometimes in fact they were only shams, as were the separate undersleeves, exposing a decorative leg below the dress, but ending above the knee. This was particularly the case with children, where all that was needed was a facade.

In women the drawers, out of modesty, were more usually hidden. Where they were lace-trimmed, the lace was in harmony with the current trend: in the early nineteenth century a simple Lille or Bucks; by the mid-century broderie anglaise; towards the end delicately patterned laces from the Leavers machine. During the third quarter of the century drawers, in the same way as petticoats, became extremely elegant garments, their fine lawn frilled and traversed with dainty bands of hand- or machine-made Valenciennes.

Combinations of camisole and drawers, or of chemise and drawers – or vest and drawers in the case of men – produced combinations. For women even these could appear seductive, trimmed with slanted insertions of lace, enriched with rivulets of the slenderest tucks and bordered with deep vandykes.

While for men nightwear, like daywear, was laceless, for women during the period of the 1870s it developed in the same way as other underwear into vastly more elegant garments. From being fairly plain and – apart from being ankle-length instead of knee-length – similar to the chemise of the day, the nightdress became intricately cut, and cleverly intersected with swathes and frillings of lace. In the late 1890s it mirrored the great shoulders and

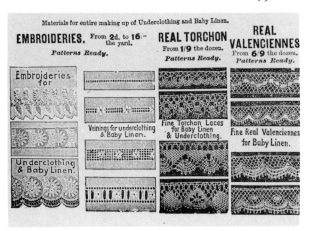

139 *Examples of simple laces and Swiss embroideries for down-market underclothing, 1890s, from Steinmann's of Piccadilly.*

swollen arms of daytime wear, and bore a super-abundance of lace.

Negligées, which had indicated an informal morning gown in the eighteenth century now became, near the end of the nineteenth, a decorative garment to be worn over a nightdress. Made of fine lawn, open down the front, with a fitted top, trailing hem, and lace engageants falling from the sleeve ends, it indeed resembled a reincarnation of the eighteenth-century nightgown, differing in little except that it was worn over a night-time nightdress instead of over a daytime shift.

Not only new garments but a whole new language for them was developing. 'Vest' changed its meaning from a waistcoat over the shirt to a warmth-providing layer worn under the shirt and next to the skin. Drawers, from their resemblance to the knickerbockers or loose-fitting breeches gathered at the knees worn by Dutchmen in New York, came in the late nineteenth century to be called knickers. The word lingerie, derived from the French *linge*, meaning linen, first appeared in the *Court Magazine* in 1835: 'It is expected that lingerie will be this season in very great request, both in morning and half-dress',[5] that is for informal and semi-formal occasions. It is unlikely that it referred to hidden garments. Further, drawings in *The Englishwoman's Domestic Magazine* of 1868 clearly label, as lingerie, little muslin jackets, jabots, cravats and chemisettes, all things that were mainly overwear, and not even linen. Its literal meaning was thus distorted from the very moment when it crept into the vocabulary of fashion. Its use as a

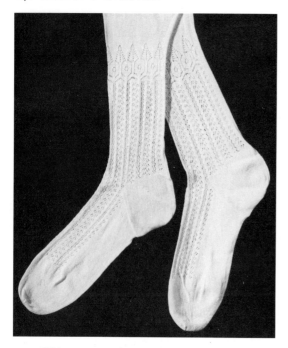

140 *White cotton stockings with lacy-knit instep and ankles, early nineteenth century.*

generic term for all ladies' underwear dates from the twentieth century.

Nineteenth-century stockings of white cotton or black silk, glimpsed beneath ankle-length muslin skirts, below swaying crinolines, or the lifted hemline of later modes, continued to favour the lacy-knit instep and lower leg which had become established in the late eighteenth century (fig. 140).

The twentieth century

The twentieth century was disrupted after only 14 years by a shattering war in the sombre light of which both fashion, and lace in fashion, must have seemed quite exceptionally frivolous. Nevertheless, during the first decade and a half a slinky elegance, begun in the last quarter of the nineteenth century, was gradually erasing all trace of the hidebound rigidity of Victorian underwear.

'Now that lace is all the rage . . .' pronounced *The Graphic* in 1900. The most exquisite petticoats, costing up to £50 a piece, were matched with remarkably pretty sleeveless camisoles, neatly shaped to the waist, and trimmed with frilled Valenciennes, and narrow bands of insertions. Camisoles, combined with drawers, had frilly shoulders, narrow waists and broad legs to around calf level where they were slotted with ribbon and

deeply vandyked with lace. This lavish harmony of beautifully cut, exquisitely finished undergarments, subtly foaming with lace, marked an artistic peak in design and inspiration.

It was the designer Poiret who slipped the constricting body shackles down from the waist to the lower legs, which he restricted within a hobble skirt. The tiny waist, near fossilized in its bony strait-jacket, was now itself at last out of fashion. Its release brought in a straighter, looser line, and the bulges and hollows of the princess petticoat were smoothed out into a slip which hung from the shoulders by narrow straps.

Tremendous efforts were made after the War to beguile lace once more into fashion. American soldiers, culling antique and modern laces from the countries they occupied, took home in 1918 a treasure trove which their women folk lost no time at all in converting into 'corsets formed of priceless old rose point, chemises encrusted with the choicest laces of Buckinghamshire, and camisoles made entirely of the rarest Alençon'.[6] Tiny fragments were built up into that sort of patchwork mélange known as Normandy lace, which consisted of cut and shaped pieces harmoniously arranged if inconsequently mingled. Its making proved a popular pastime, and underwear, modesties, boudoir caps and nightcaps were all trimmed with it.

During the 1920s, the replacement of white lawn undies with pastel-coloured silks accelerated. Ecru-tinted laces formed edgings, insertions and incrustations upon chemises – which now meant slip-like petticoats shortening over a few years from mid-calf to above the knee, and cami-knickers, the diminutive spawn of the nineteenth-century linen combinations.

For the upper levels of society the Belgian bobbin lace of Antwerp, Bruges flower lace and point de fée, all well made in a firm and creamy cotton thread, decorated the upper and lower borders of these various garments, which were now often made in sets matched for colour and fabric. Hand-embroidered Richelieu work on pure silk was also popular. Machine imitations of prestigious laces were exact and near indistinguishable. They even borrowed names such as Alençon and Chantilly, though these were not always in any way appropriate. 'Cut-out' machine laces were especially designed for underwear. They consisted in effect of collections of motifs lightly joined by easily severed

(c)

strands, so that the self-contained medallions could then be applied at will.

The favourite fabrics of the 1920s and '30s were rayon, crêpe de chine and silk milanese. This latter was, if not a lace, at least a cellular fabric closely related to warp-knitted laces. The stitches were slanted sideways in two opposing directions so that lightness of weight, stoutness of texture and resilience in wear were all combined. Silk tricots were also popular, and also made on the warp-knitting machine. Like the milanese they used two sets of warps, and so produced a double fabric, but the vertical lines of loops, instead of being passed diagonally through the whole width of the material, were lapped only from one wale to the next, then back again, in a R–L R–L manner. In other words, while the front warps were slanted to the right, the back were slanted to the left, so that a strong, elastic, air-containing fabric was produced which combined warmth, smoothness and lack of bulk. Other warp knits could be easily adapted for openwork patterning, and so approximated more closely to laces.

142 *(a) Open drawers, c.1860.*
(b) 'Combinations', 1922.
(c) Boudoir caps, chemises, combinations and negligée, 1925.
(d) Shoulder straps and the flat-chested look in cami-knickers, c.1928.

Apart from imitations of Belgian laces, the Leavers machine could produce tiers of cobwebby lace so soft it had almost no thickness. Such flounces were made of silk or art silk (artificial silk of acetate or viscose rayons) which, though invented considerably earlier, only came extensively on to the market at the end of the third decade. They were attached to the slips at waist level, and hung down to a knee-length hem. Lacy-knits in wool, or in cotton-and-wool mixtures, were aimed at the lower end of the market, with matching vests, slips, knickers and combinations.

Some firms provided, so that girls could make their own trousseaux, kits which contained ready-to-sew garments of silk or rayon underwear, tog-

43 *Stockings with insertions of lace down the shin, worn with a skimpy camisole, and drawers with elastic at the knees and a lace incrustation on the thigh, c.1928.*

Slip and Scanties, 10,685—3/-

144 *1957:(a) A cotton half slip frilled with Schiffli-embroidered nylon.*
(b) Slip and scanties.

ether with all the lace needed to decorate them. The gist of the accompanying commercials was that a bride's entire future happiness depended on her having all her underwear covered in lace.

Stockings of this period, as earlier in the century, might well have actual lace insertions extending down the front lower leg and across the foot. This amazingly spendthrift affectation put black Chantilly into black silk stockings, and superb quality Alençon dyed to match its flesh-pink hose (fig. 143).

During the Second World War (1939–45) the manufacture of lace was stopped, as contributing nothing to the national interest. This gap in continuity, and the loss of experienced and skilled workers, made it difficult for the machine-lace industry of the 1940s to recover. Cotton waist slips frilled with broderie anglaise were embroidered on the Schiffli machine. Bouffant layers of nylon net puffed out the skirts of short evening gowns. Indeed patterned lace fabrics and plain nets were equally welcomed, during the period of clothes rationing, because they needed no coupons.

The further development of man-made fibres, and of a revitalized warp-knitting machine known as the Raschel, brought a new style of 'intimate apparel' onto the market, from the 1960s. Micro-mesh tights, or pantyhose, were composed of a fabric of uniform but complexly integrated meshes, and lent themselves easily to larger scale patterning.

Elasticated laces, using natural Lastex fibres, appeared shortly before 1934 under the trade name

E-lace-tic. The synthetic Lycra, with the same qualities of expansion and recoil, but greater durability, revolutionized the controlling aspect of underwear with lightweight lacy-knit fabrics, or delicately patterned bobbinets. The old rigidity of the all-containing corsets disappeared as they split into top (brassiere) and bottom (suspender-belt or girdle) until by the 1980s they began to appear like glamourized fig leaves from the garden of Eden (fig. 145).

The revival of interest in old lace for overwear, c.1970, brought, in the general turning-out of that period, a great quantity of Victorian and Edwardian white underwear onto the market. These garments were converted for overwear, long petticoats being

145 *The graceful unrestricting bra and suspender belt of the 1980s, minimally tightened with Lycra bobbinet, and making effective use of a machine-lace edging. Berlei* Gypsy *range.*

146 *French knickers and camisole with a pretty Leavers lace trim. Berlei* Je t'aime *range, 1980s.*

worn as skirts, camisoles as tops, chemises as dresses, and drawers as blouses with legs converted into arms. Some of them were very lacy indeed, and their easy availability revived an interest in the wearing of lace.

Yet more broderie anglaise was made on the Schiffli machine during a brief ethnic phase of fashion in the 1970s. It trimmed white cotton petticoats which were intended to show, peasant-wise, beneath mid-calf woollen skirts.

However, during the 1960s and '70s the tendency to wear fewer clothes during the day, combined with more efficient heating of houses at night, reduced the function of underwear as a warmth provider, while the easy-care laundering of clothes in general annihilated its protective function. Its function of changing the body shape was rendered superfluous by a more realistic appraisal of flesh, and by more enlightened diets, as well as by fashions for tight jeans, thigh-length skirts and topless dresses which between them revealed all the secrets of the human form. Thus, while in the nineteenth century it would have been customary for all the items of underwear to be put on, it would be not

entirely unusual in the later twentieth century for them all to be left off.

Only the function of visible enhancement remained, and this without doubt lace could supply (fig. 146). But a source of lace was difficult to find. Hand laces could not be made commercially except in the Far East and these, though well made, were too heavy for dainty silk and synthetic fabrics. Machine laces in the post-War period suffered from poor design, not so much through lack of designers as through lack of the expected financial return needed to translate them into threads. Once a demi-glamour market has been established, and attempts made to upgrade it, manufacturers could invest in more effective designs such as those used by Janet Reger for her half-slips, bras, briefs and nighties which, though delightful to look at, were at between £100 and £500 a piece not entirely viable commercially.

It remains to be seen whether machines, still capable of producing laces with all the visual impact of those ravishing creations of the past, can afford to do so.

8

Peasant Laces

SUBSTANCE AND SHADOW

Peasant laces, together with those made for the church, and for furnishing, were the stout substance from which the ethereal fashion laces sprang, and back into which they withdrew some 300 years later. Their firm foundation lay in earthy needs (fig. 147). They were utilitarian and functional, their decorative qualities robust and open. These archaic forms of braids, macramé, drawnwork and netting persisted beneath the evanescent mists of fashion.

What we know of them during that long time is thrown into shadow by the splendour above. Peasant laces were not fashion in the defined sense. The poor were severely restricted by law in the clothes they were allowed to wear: 'No servant to husbandry, nor common labourer ... shall wear in their clothing any cloth whereof the broad yard shall exceed in price 11s [55p] ...' (1482).[1] What remains of them are surviving examples without provenance, country or date – until the mid-nineteenth century; and a series of names such as Colbertine, Bisette and Gueuse, cropping up in literary and other references which give us little information as to their appearance or their construction. Even in paintings they were not shown clearly, since only the rich seemed able to elicit from artists a minute attention to the details of their apparel.

The early pattern books, especially for bobbin laces (Venice 1557 and Zurich 1561) show collections of peasant laces on their way to becoming transfigured by the use of richer thread and more complex designs into something acceptable to fashion. Many of the patterns are for small numbers of bobbins such as 8, 12 or 16. Few require more than 60.

The stolid continuity of such laces, through hundreds of years, contrasts sharply with the change and flow of texture, technique and design within the glorious creations of the world above. The subdued simplicity of peasant laces gives them not so much an anachronistic quality as a timeless one: they are not behind the times but apart from them.

It is unlikely that they were made by dedicated or intensely hard-working professionals as were the fashion laces; it is more likely that girls and housewives worked them in their spare time. So their construction had to be suited to the limited time available, and to the abilities of the maker. Needle laces were inappropriate: to achieve the even tension of row upon row of small buttonhole stitches, the threads needed to be held firmly, and constantly pressed with the thumb, which was no

147 *The bavolet, the simple peasant cap of the early sixteenth century, which later inspired the fontange and lappets of the aristocracy. Holbein, 1527. Its form persisted in nineteenth-century caps worn by peasant women of the province of Saintonge.*

job for work-roughened fingers. For the working
classes a heavy drawnwork, or a bobbin lace made
in thickish thread, was more expedient, being
speedy to make yet of suitably impressive
appearance.

In Scandinavia, women who worked in the fields
could carry with them small pieces of cloth
stretched over birch bark and, as opportunity arose,
embroider them with openwork to make trimmings
for marriage shirts or household linens. The bobbin
lace pillow required a more sedentary situation,
such as a mother at home with her children. Patterns
were frequently geometric, worked at a 45° angle, as
were torchon laces. Wool or stout linen thread
might be used or, after the 1830s, cotton. In the
nineteenth century the use of horsehair, or straw, or
a combination of the two, was typical of the canton
of Argovia in Switzerland, and some was also made
near Neuchâtel (fig. 148).[2] A sinuous trail and bright
colours occurred in East European peasant laces,
such as those of Russia and Hungary.

More complex and slowly worked laces, with a
Lille or point de Paris ground, were highly valued
for peasant bonnets in France, the Netherlands and
other largely agricultural countries (fig. 149). Compared with the size of the women's incomes, they
were extremely expensive and, though they lacked
the ephemeral quality of fashion laces, they were the
object of that same avid covetousness, and desire to
outshine all others, which burnt the heart, and
fingers, of the aristocracy. They were, however,
expected to endure at least a lifetime.

The invention of Heathcoat's bobbinets opened
up new possibilities. The designs of bobbin laces
such as Lille and Tønder could be imitated with
scrupulous exactitude by using a simple running
stitch which passed in and out of the meshes, or
using a chain stitch made with a tambour hook. The
finer provincial bonnets of this period often mingle
such embroidered nets with their bobbin lace
prototypes, and the two are scarcely distinguishable
from each other except by close examination.
Embroidered nets were also used as christening
veils (fig. 150).

Copies of bobbin laces were also made on the
Leavers machine, and worn on French provincial
bonnets from the mid-nineteenth century. Similar
copies, made on the Schiffli machine, were occasionally used for peasant skirts and aprons of the early
twentieth century.

Domestic, or non-professional, lace-makers,
working at home but dependent on that income to
support themselves, were usually unable to spare
the money to keep for themselves the lace they so
assiduously produced (fig. 151).

(a)

(b)

148 (a) An Icelandic peasant skirt decorated with bobbin lace in red and green wool, nineteenth century.

(b) A torchon-type lace of horsehair decorated with finely plaited undulating ropes of straw. Made at Val-de-Travers, mid-nineteenth century.

Two other aspects of non-fashion or sub-fashion laces may be mentioned here. Firstly, servants of the rich and noble occupied a privileged position in being the recipients of outmoded laces discarded by their employers. In addition, many of the upper servants, or courtiers, in the royal Court, were themselves noble, and so wore fashion laces in their own right (fig. 152). Others stole, to acquire what they wanted. Pepys, on 2 September 1667, reported:

After dinner came in Mr Townsend [Clerk of the Great Wardrobe], and there I was witness of a horrid rateing which Mr Ashburnham, as one of the Grooms of the King's bedchamber, did give him for want of linen for the King's person; which he swore was not to be endured, and that the King would not endure it, and that the King his father [Charles I] would have hanged his Wardrobe-man should he have been served so; the King having at this day no handkerchers, and but three bands [collars, probably lace rabats] to his neck. Mr Townsend pleaded want of money and the owing of the linen-draper 5000£; and that it was the Grooms taking away the King's linen at the quarter's end, as their fees, which makes this great want.

Fashion laces were certainly valuable enough to be worth the effort of stealing. Defoe in *Moll Flanders*, published in 1722, makes his lowly-born heroine steal a parcel of bone lace worth nearly £20; and on another occasion £300-worth of Flanders lace, though this she had to share with a dishonest Customs official, since it should not have been allowed into England, its importation being prohibited.

Secondly, lace-making of all kinds was adopted as a hobby, or non-commercial pastime for many women during the second half of the nineteenth century. The types of lace covered an enormous range, from craft to bobbin and needle. The accessories thus created were a kind of fashion, even if not of the highest mode. An Australian journal of 1912 even illustrated a lace pillow set up with bobbins and pricking, describing it as 'The New Princess Lace Machine' for the 'Beautiful Art of Lace Making. No teacher needed. Ladies, earn money at home. The latest invention.' (Fig. 153.) The advertisement continued: 'For use in making fine Torchon, Valenciennes, Cluny, Smyrna, Brussels, Honiton, Medici and Duchess. Our new method is the most perfect in existence, and can be learnt by a child.' (*Everybody's Journal*.)

Finally, in the sub-fashion world of the professional classes and public servants, traditional or ceremonial dress, with its laces, lingered on as though to chase capricious fashion would pose

149 *(a) Lace made in Beveren for provincial bonnets,*
twentieth century, using older designs.
  (b) A starched provincial bonnet of decorated net.
A. van Hamme, nineteenth century.

some threat to their solidity (fig. 154). Lawyers retained collars in the shape of rabats; Speakers of the House wore lace cravats. Wenceslaus Hollar's engraving, dated 1645, of the wife of the Lord Mayor of London (fig. 155) shows her wearing a ruff, already in England 15 years out of date.

The provincial well-to-do on the other hand chased vigorously, having a tendency to out-London London, catching the wave of fashion as it passed and launching themselves upon it to create a local splash (fig. 156).

Lace existed long before it became fashion, but it was fashion which miraculously transformed its techniques into a perfection of thread-movements

150 *A Bavarian peasant christening. A little veil of embroidered net is spread over the swaddled baby. The mother wears a lace collar. Johann Sperl (1840–1914).*

151 *(a) A Bedfordshire lace school, c.1900. The teacher wears magnifying spectacles. The huge pillow for continuous laces has not changed in style over 300 years.*

(b) More light-hearted workers, perhaps less dependent on their earnings. The relatively large size of the bobbins, in the basket and on the floor, suggests a semi-coarse lace. Van Loo, seventeenth century.

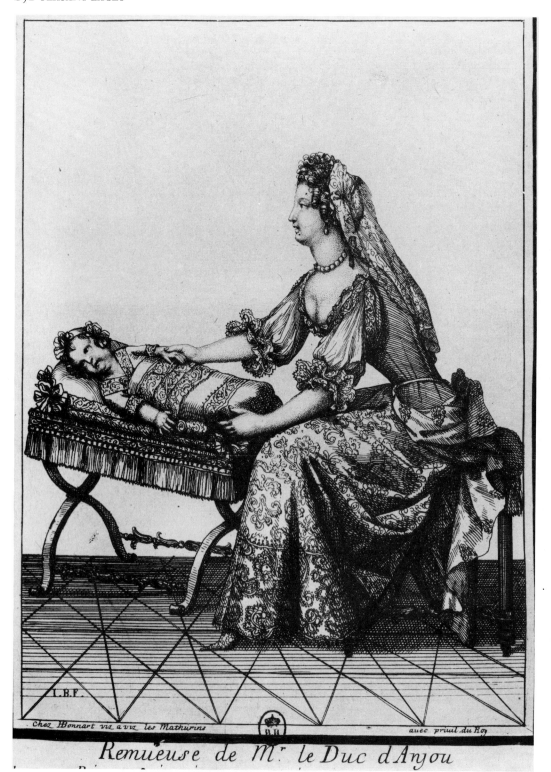

Remüeuse de M.^r le Duc d'Anjou

152 *The 'rocker' of The Duke of Anjou (born 1683)*
would be a noble lady. She wears lace on her chemise neck
and elbows. The sleeves of her gown have been removed.

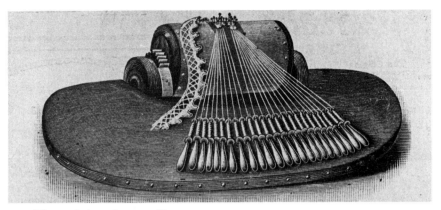

153 *The new Princess Lace machine, 1912.*

154 *(a) A simple, unobtrusive lace is worn by the garden designer John Tradescant the Younger. Attributed to E. de Critz, 1652. It resembles a Cluny furnishing lace, such as forms the edges and seams of the late seventeenth-century winding sheet (fig. 154(b)).*

155 *The wife of the Lord Mayor of London wearing a ruff some 15 years after it had been superseded in fashion by the falling collar. Wenceslaus Hollar, 1646.*

156 *Bourgeois fashion: all that glitters is not gold. All the paraphernalia is to present a brave show, to solicit credit, and to imitate the nobility. Her fontange tilts forward, the lappets hang, the cap back is frilled, and petticoat and mantle have gathered flounces of lace, 1690.*

and designs of surpassing beauty and transcendent skill. That such laces could ever exist, and that some have survived, is our good fortune. Only bad social conditions, embodying a form of slave labour, ever made them possible on a large commercial scale. With improvements in conditions that conjugation passed, and antique laces are no longer replaceable.

It is thus of immense importance not only that all actual surviving pieces of lace from the past should be cherished, but also that lace-makers, by actively perpetuating the ancient techniques, should preserve for posterity our knowledge of how they were made.

A Note on Money

The present-day equivalent of sixteenth-century and later currencies is of vital importance to a study of lace in fashion since only by turning the quoted costs into familiar terms can we appreciate their expense.

It is, however, extremely difficult even to attempt a simple conversion. Throughout the ages prices of goods did not rise and fall in unison, nor did they have any consistent relation to wages for different types of work. While some went up others went down, and thus even to select a fully reliable standard for comparison is in itself almost impossible, and widely varying multiples can be recommended depending on which standard the author has chosen – bread, wages, rents, cost of land etc.

Coulton in *The Meaning of Medieval Moneys* suggests a ×6 increase for the years from 1450 to 1707; and a ×40 from the thirteenth century to 1931. Porter recommends that, starting with the eighteenth century, we should multiply by 60 for a 1982 equivalent.

In industrial England of the nineteenth and twentieth centuries the situation becomes very complex indeed. Ivan Fallan in the *Sunday Times* of 5 September 1982 suggested that the purchasing power of the £ sterling fell from 67.91p in 1931 to 3.54p in 1982 (taking 1914 as £1 = 100p), i.e. there was a ×20 cost of living increase in these 50 years. Similarly a function of 39.5 would be required to convert prices of 1896 to a 1982 equivalence.

Two examples quoted in the *Sunday Times* demonstrate the nature of the problem very clearly:

(a) A *general* purchasing power of £225 in 1851 would be equivalent to £6,500 in 1982 (a factor of ×28.95). However, a house costing £225 in 1851 would in fact cost £30,000 in 1982, though varying a bit according to the part of England considered.
(b) In 1882 the *general* purchasing power of £1 was 100.08p, compared with 3.54p in 1982, a cost of living increase of ×28.27. Thus coal at 18s 6d (92.5p) a ton in 1882 should have cost £26 in 1982. In fact it cost £84.

Conclusion: all multiples of this kind must be treated as postulates, not facts.

To give one lace example: if the general purchasing power of £1 in 1840 is taken as 77.91p (*Sunday Times*), a multiple of 22 is needed to estimate the 1982 value, making the cost of Queen Victoria's wedding lace £22,000.

Foreign currencies were at least as complex as those of England, since each varied in its own particular way. Snelling, writing in 1766 says 'There is no part of Europe where their money has remained so long fixed and unchanged in its value as in England, where the Silver has continued of the same value within a trifle for 200 years ...' (i.e. since Elizabeth I's reform of the currency in 1560, page 14). But many countries such as France and Spain underwent rapid and extensive changes; and some from time to time were so unfavourable that neighbouring countries refused to deal in them. 'Prussian currency is 14% worse than Leipzig,' says Snelling; and 'There is always some confusion in the coins of Germany.'

Pleasant therefore as it would be to include here a short list of the main coins in circulation during the sixteenth to twentieth centuries, and their English equivalents, the amount of space required to do it at all pedantically would be absolutely enormous.

As a very rough guide, then, in the text a multiple of 35 to 40 has been used to update antique values. This represents in all cases a (somewhat) minimal amount.

The following list of coins has been adapted from Snelling. The decimal values are straight conversions of the £.s.d equivalents for foreign currencies which he quoted in 1766, and these can be updated by applying a multiple of not less than 35.

France (1726–1766)

Gold:	Louis	24 livres (later, francs)
	Ecu d'or/crown	5 livres
Silver:	Ecu d'argent	3 livres (App. 22 livres = £1)

Flanders (Austrian/Spanish Netherlands)
Gold:

Double sovereign	51 schillings	
Guinea	38 schillings	
Pistole	30 schillings	
Ducat	16 schillings	
	(1 schilling	
	$= 6\frac{3}{4}$d $= 2.8$p)	

Silver:

Ducatone	10 schillings
Croone	9 schillings

Copper and Billon (debased silver):

Sous	$\frac{1}{2}$d	
Denier	$\frac{1}{8}$d	(12d = 5p)

Bavaria and *Austria*
Silver:

Rix dollar	90 kreutzer
Dollar	60 kreutzer
Florin	30 kreutzer $= 12\frac{1}{2}$p

Germany
Gold:

Gulden	$c.35$p
Ducat	$47\frac{1}{2}$p
Pistole	83p

Silver:

Dollar	$16\frac{1}{2}$p

Russia
Gold:

Ducat	$c.40$p ('whose value is seldom the same long together' – Snelling)

Silver:

Ruble	$c.17\frac{1}{2}$p

Spain
Gold:

Pistole/doblon	83p
Escudo	$41\frac{1}{2}$p

Silver:

Piece of eight/doble/dubloon	23p
Peseta	4.6p
Ryal/real/vellon	1.3p

'In the year 1737 great alterations were made in the value of the money in Spain.' (Snelling).

Portugal
In 1688 there was an increase of 20 per cent in the nominal value of the coin, and in 1766 'none of the pieces of gold or silver are current at the value struck upon them.'

Gold:

Joannes	90p
Crusade/crown	13.5p

Silver:

Testoon/teston	2.5p

Copper:

Rees. 1000 rees (milrees)	28.5p

Italy
Each major city had its own currency. In Genoa there was a difference of 15 per cent between the value of the currency in the bank and out of the bank.

Gold:

Occhelo (4 zecchine)	£1.93 (Venice)
Doppia/pistole	92p (Genoa), 83p (Milan), 68p (Lucca)
Zecchine	48p

Silver:

Scudo d'argento	35p (Genoa), $27\frac{1}{2}$p (Venice), 28p (Milan), 23p (Lucca)
Justiniano (Venice)	$24\frac{1}{2}$p
Ducat/ducatello	$17\frac{1}{2}$p
Lire	3.3p (Milan, Lucca)

Billon:

$1\frac{1}{2}$ Lire pieces (Venice)	3.3p

Ragusa
'We are not so clear in relation to these coins as we could wish.' (Snelling).

Approx: 40 Gross = 1 Ducat = 9p. The Ragusa ducat was equivalent to that of Venetian Dalmatia, but worth only half that of Venice itself.

Glossary

Alençon a French needle lace with a reseau ground, originating *c.*1717, and fashionable to the early twentieth century.

All-overs machine laces made in yardages like dress materials, and patterned all over.

Appliqué work the stitching of design motifs to an openwork ground, either hand- or machine-made, to form a lace.

Argentan a French needle lace with a reseau ground heavier and more imposing than Alençon, popular for portraits through the eighteenth century.

Ayrshire work/flowerin' a combination of fine surface embroidery and openwork, in white, on muslin or lawn baby gowns, nineteenth century.

Barmen a machine which makes braids, and excellent copies of laces such as torchon and cluny, nineteenth–twentieth centuries.

Bath lace Bath Brussels, a non-continuous bobbin lace made in south-west England, second half of the eighteenth century, usually as large flounces, in imitation of the Brussels laces of Flanders.

Bertha a collar encircling the shoulders, leaving them bare above, or covered by a translucent tippet of gauze, muslin or lawn, seventeen–twentieth centuries.

Biggin a baby's close-fitting cap, sixteenth century.

Blonde a continuous bobbin lace using two thicknesses of thread, heavy and lustrous for the design, light and cobwebby for the reseau ground. Mid-eighteenth–mid-nineteenth centuries.

Bobbin lace a lace made of many threads which are crossed and twisted together. Weights called bobbins are hung from the threads, and hold a reserve around their necks. The bobbins were originally of bone (hence bone lace), and the work is supported on a cushion or pillow (hence pillow lace).

Bobbinet a machine net invented by John Heathcoat in 1808, and based on Bucks point ground.

Bone lace lace made with bobbins (*see also* Bobbin lace).

Boot hose short socks worn inside boots to prevent their contact with the silk stockings covering the legs, seventeenth century.

Boudoir cap an indoor cap, lace-trimmed, and worn with a negligée, basically to cover untidy hair, twentieth century.

Bouillon little swellings puffing out the fabric of a dress, like the steam bubbles of boiling water, nineteenth century.

Brabantine of the province of Brabant in east Flanders (capital, Brussels).

Broderie anglaise/Madeira work an embroidered lace made by punching holes in cloth (usually white cotton) and embroidering around them, mid-nineteenth century.

Brussels non-continuous bobbin laces associated with the area around Brussels, in Belgium, formerly Flanders, seventeenth–twentieth centuries; also decorated nets from that area, nineteenth–twentieth centuries.

Bucks point a continuous bobbin lace made in the East Midlands of England, and having a reseau (mesh) ground, seventeenth–twentieth centuries.

Buratto a plain gauze (leno) weave, which could be decorated with running stitches to make an embroidered lace, mainly fifteenth–seventeenth centuries.

Canions/canons lace or ribbon decorations of the knees or lower legs of men, sometimes attached to the boot hose, seventeenth century.

Cap back the teacosy-shaped piece of lace which formed the back of the commode *c.*1682–1712. Later it moved to the top of the head, and the tall fontange became a small gathered frill at its front, eighteenth century.

Carrickmacross a lace formed by shapes of woven fabric applied to a net ground (appliqué) or joined by strands of thread (guipure), mid-nineteenth–twentieth centuries.

Chantilly a French continuous bobbin lace made of matt silk, usually black, the design in halfstitch, *c.*1750–1900.

Chemical lace machine embroidery on a fabric which is later destroyed, leaving only the compacted embroidery stitches as a 'burnt' or 'chemical' lace. Began commercially in the 1880s.

Chevaux de frize lappets lappets with a vandyked or scalloped border, eighteenth century.

Chevex lace literally hair lace, a ribbon for tying up the hair, eighteenth century.

Chitterling a lace frill down the front of a man's shirt, seventeenth–eighteenth centuries.

Cluny a continuous bobbin lace characterized by divided trails, sixteenth–twentieth centuries; a form with long leaves (oval point d'esprits) revived in France and England after 1850.

Colberteen a coarse woollen bobbin lace made in France and copied in England, seventeenth–eighteenth centuries.

Colobium sindonis a simple short-sleeved white gown worn under the rich supertunica at a monarch's coronation.

Commode/fontange/tower/head originally more specific, these became general terms for the build-up of hair, wire, lace, ribbon etc. as a tiered fontage, cap back and paired lappets, worn mainly at Court, *c.*1682–1712.

Continuous bobbin lace lace in which the threads of the design pass into the openwork ground and back again, i.e. design and ground are worked in continuity.

Cornely machine a machine used for embroidery on net (or other fabrics) often using chain stitch in coloured silks, nineteenth–twentieth centuries.

Craft lace laces usually made at home, by non-professionals, and in a time-saving manner, e.g. crochet, knitting, tatting etc, mainly mid-nineteenth century and after.

Cravat a linen scarf tied round the neck, with the loose ends at the front often made of lace (fig. 45), seventeenth–eighteenth centuries.

Crochet (a) lace built up of chain stitches worked with a crochet hook; (b) Irish crochet – a very fine, complex and often three-dimensional form of crochet, with a design of flowers and a guipure ground. Both mainly mid-nineteenth–twentieth centuries.

Cutwork an embroidered lace formed by the removal of shapes of woven linen, most commonly small squares, then using the spaces as frames within which decorative patterns of buttonhole stitches could be built up, mainly sixteenth–seventeenth centuries.

Devon lace a non-continuous bobbin lace produced mainly around Honiton and Beer, seventeenth–twentieth centuries.

Drawnwork the drawing together, or out, of threads from a plain weave fabric to make an openwork, i.e. a form of embroidered lace.

Dresden an exceptionally fine form of drawnwork, made in Saxony, with many variations of stitches, usually mingled with surface embroidery, mid-eighteenth century.

Droschel a bobbin lace ground, consisting of minute hexagonal meshes, two sides of each mesh being made of four threads plaited together four times, and characteristic of the Brussels laces of the late seventeenth to early nineteenth centuries.

Duchesse a non-continuous bobbin lace made at centres near Brussels, and often having needle lace inclusions, nineteenth-twentieth centuries.

Ecru an unbleached, or darkened colour, like a deep cream or pale coffee, popular for lace in the early and late nineteenth century.

Engageants cuffs: (a) asymmetrically shaped to fall deeply below the elbows in two or three rows, eighteenth century; (b) frills within the sleeve ends, or entire undersleeves extending from elbow to wrist, nineteenth century.

En tablier in the shape of an apron extending downwards, and sometimes upwards, from the waist.

Eschelles scales as in fish, or broad scallops around a skirt, an effect achieved by catching the fabric of a flounce together at intervals, nineteenth century.

Fichu nineteenth century, called a *tippet* seventeenth–eighteenth centuries; a close-fitting cape of lightweight material, usually triangular, with the apex down the back and the front ends knotted together or crossed at the waist.

Filet a net made of square meshes knotted at every corner, usually decorated by running or darning stitches to make an embroidered lace.

Flounce a deep layer of lace attached to the garment along one of its sides and hanging free at the other.

Flowerin' see *Ayrshire*.

Fly a lady's cap of lace or gauze wired out at the sides like small wings, and garnished with jewels, for formal occasions 1750s–60s.

Fontange see *Commode*.

Frenched hair cut short and curled round the face (fig. 69).

Furbelow showy pleats or gathers of fabric on a skirt or petticoat.

Gadrooned fluted compactly like the periphery of a millstone ruff.

Gimp/gympt a lace of simple design, of gold or silver thread, intended to be sewn flat onto the fabric in the manner of a braid (fig. 133a).

Godet triangular insertions of fabric or lace in the hem of a skirt to give added decorative fullness, late nineteenth century.

Gollila a flat collar going right round the neck, and stiffly starched so that it projected above the shoulders, seventeenth century (fig. 27).

Ground the openwork part of a lace, as distinct from the design.

Guipure a lace in which the openwork ground is not a series of tiny uniform meshes (reseau) but an irregular arrangement of bars linking the various parts of the design. It thus includes an enormous variety of laces, both hand and machine, and was sometimes used to indicate the chemical laces as a whole.

Halfstitch in bobbin laces a stitch in which the threads are not closely compacted so that the design appears lightweight and like a miniature trelliswork.

Hand machine a Swiss embroidery machine worked entirely by hand and foot power, its products almost indistinguishable from those made by hand, nineteenth–twentieth centuries.

Honiton a non-continuous bobbin lace made in various parts of Devon, seventeenth–twentieth centuries.

Incrustations lace medallions, often thick and three-dimensional, to be sewn on or into blouses or underwear, nineteenth–twentieth centuries.

Insertions lengths of lace, straight on both sides, and let into garments for decorative purposes (i.e. like a seaming lace but with a different function).

Jabot a bunch of lace attached to the bodice or shirt at the front, rather than round the neck like a cravat, nineteenth–twentieth centuries.

Jacquard a patterning device consisting of a series, sometimes hundreds, of punched cards which control the movements of threads and thus the designs of machine laces (and woven fabrics), invented 1801.

Jupon an underskirt, or fancy petticoat, revealed by an elegantly caught-up overskirt, as in the eighteenth century, 1860s.

Kerchief/handkerchief/tippet see Fichu.

Lacemen lace merchants and dealers, the middle-men linking maker and customer, seventeenth–nineteenth centuries.

Lappets streamers of lace from the head, their length for Court prescribed by social status, late seventeenth–nineteenth centuries; also used of the ear pieces of everyday fall caps, and for small scarves, the shape of two joined lappets, second half of the nineteenth century.

Leavers a twist net machine which could make extremely complex designs, invented 1813.

Loom laces woven laces created on small looms by the hand-manipulation of weft threads, seventeenth century and after.

Looped net, or looped lace a plain or patterned fabric knitted on the Stocking Frame, or Warp Frame, machines, 1760s and after.

Macramé a lace made by many threads being selectively knotted together.

Madeira work see *Broderie anglaise*.

Maltese a continuous bobbin lace from Malta, usually of pale gold or black silk, and bearing the Maltese cross. Also used of East Midlands copies, in cotton or linen, known as Beds Maltese, after 1850.

Malines/Mechlin/Macklin/Mechelen a continuous bobbin lace from around Mechelen in Flanders, eighteenth–nineteenth centuries. Also used generically for all Flemish bobbin laces, seventeenth century.

Milanese fabric a closely textured knitted fabric made on the Warp Frame machine, and on a variety of Raschel, nineteenth–twentieth centuries.

Milanese lace a non-continuous bobbin lace from north Italy, late sixteenth–mid-eighteenth centuries, often used on ecclesiastical vestments.

Needle lace a single-thread lace built up of various kinds of buttonhole stitching.

Net a machine-made ground of small uniform meshes. *Twist net* – the meshes are made by the threads being twisted around each other. *Patent net* – used of machine-made looped or knitted nets, to distinguish them from the hand-made droschels: the name died out soon after the invention of bobbinet (twist net) in 1808.

Nightgown / deshabille / negligée / undress / morning dress / half-dress / demi-toilette a reasonably comfortable and semi-relaxed though often quite splendid dress, for less formal occasions, seventeenth–eighteenth centuries (fig. 47).

Non-continuous bobbin lace a lace in which the design elements are made individually, and subsequently connected by a meshwork (reseau) or by a series of bars of thread (guipure).

Pardessus a little fitted jacket, hip length, and trimmed with lace, nineteenth century.

Partlet it has several meanings, one being a simple ruff, at first part of the shirt or chemise, later a separate accessory, mid-sixteenth century.

Passement a straight-edged lace, sometimes of silk or linen thread, a forerunner of scalloped or dentate edgings, sixteenth–seventeenth centuries.

Pelerine a small shoulder cape with long ties or hanging pieces at the front, in the nineteenth century often of lace, or embroidered muslin.

Pelisse a loose-fitting cloak for adults or children, sometimes with slits for the arms, seventeenth–eighteenth centuries; later made of, or trimmed with, lace, and sometimes long and semi-shaped like a negligée, having a train, and worn over a nightdress, late nineteenth century.

Picots little loops along the heading of a lace, or decorating parts of the design.

Pinner 'the lappet of a head [i.e. commode] which flies loose' (Johnson, 1755).

Plaited lace a bobbin lace, usually Genoese, where the design is built up in a geometric manner from plaited strands to look rather like a punto in aria, sixteenth–seventeenth centuries.

Plastron a breastplate, or cover to the front opening of a bodice, stylishly shaped and often continuing upwards into a choker collar, made of laces such as Beds Maltese or Honiton, late nineteenth century.

Point/renaissance/tape/braid lace a craft lace using straight machine, or bobbin-made, braids to outline a design which was then joined, and filled in, with varieties of buttonhole stitches, post-1850.

Point d'Angleterre a seventeenth- and eighteenth-century Brussels bobbin lace, non-continuous and of great delicacy, usually with a fine droschel ground.

Point d'Espagne a needle lace of luxuriant design, three-dimensional and associated with Spain but possibly made to commission in Venice, second half of the seventeenth century.

Point de fée a continuous bobbin lace, a twentieth-century form of Binche.

Point de France a French needle lace of neatly symmetrical rococo detail, started in 1664 by Louis XIV and Colbert, ended *c.*1700.

Point de gaze a delicate Belgian needle lace associated with Brussels; the flowers have raised petals, and the ground resembling a fine gauze though made of buttonhole stitches, nineteenth–twentieth centuries.

Point de Paris/wire ground/Kat stitch the ground of a French lace, used in the East Midlands at the time of the Napoleonic wars.

Point de Venise/Venetian gros point a needle lace of great beauty and work so fine that even with a magnifying glass it is difficult to see the stitches, three-dimensional with a design of large flowers, *c.*1650–1700.

Punto in aria a needle lace of scalloped or toothed form, antedating the development of national characteristics in needle laces. It was the earliest type to be made independently of a woven fabric, i.e. to be a true needle, rather than an embroidered, lace, sixteenth–seventeenth centuries.

Purling a border to early coifs and ruffs looking like crescents of scales piled up on each other, made with a needle, often of gold thread, sixteenth century.

Pusher a twist-net machine making excellent imitations of Chantilly shawls in the 1850s and '60s, and later stoles of shiny Chinese silk, ended *c.*1910.

Rabat a bib-like collar worn with a periwig, and made of linen trimmed with lace, or entirely of lace; similar shapes sometimes worn by infants (fig. 43), mid-seventeenth century.

Raschel a warp-knitting machine developed in the 1950s. It works extremely quickly, and uses synthetic fibre.

Reseau a lace ground with the openwork made of regular meshes, in a variety of ways.

Reticella a lace similar to cutwork but made not inside a framework of woven cloth but of plaited or needlewoven strands. The same patterns could be used, but the amount of labour was reduced, *c.*1600 and on.

Robing bands of fabric or lace attached on either side of an open bodice or skirt, or on a closed skirt to give the impression that it was open, mainly eighteenth century.

Ruff originally a circular collar standing out narrowly from the neck and fluted in a figure-of-eight manner. *Millstone ruff*: a wider form, some 20 inches in diameter, often edged with purling or punto in aria and embroidered with cutwork, *c.*1575–1625.

Ruffles sleeve frills at elbow or wrist, when large called engageants; when like tiny millstones, called ruff-cuffs. Sixteenth–nineteenth centuries.

Schiffli an embroidery machine using two sets of threads (needle and shuttle). It can embroider a net to imitate a reseaud lace, or a disposable fabric to imitate a guipure, 1880s and on.

Seaming lace a utilitarian lace joining widths of fabric together (fig. 134), seventeenth century and earlier.

Sewings in non-continuous bobbin laces the picking up of threads around the outer borders of the motifs in order to make the ground, e.g. droschel.

Shoe roses rosettes of lace worn of the shoes, of variable size and often of precious metal, early seventeenth century.

Sortie de bal something lacy to put over the shoulders when leaving the ball, second half of the nineteenth century.

Sprang a technique for twisting together strands of thread fixed in a framework like a small loom. A primitive openwork technique, not much used for fashion laces.

Sprigging/sprigged muslin tambour decoration in the form of tiny, simple, scattered flowers, late eighteenth/early nineteenth centuries.

Steinkirk a cravat, usually lace-ended, which was looped up through a buttonhole to keep it from flopping about, ended 1720.

Stocking Frame a machine invented in the late sixteenth century for knitting stockings and similar garments. Adapted for the making of nets and lace from the 1760s.

Stole a long scarf of hand-made lace, or decorated net, popular *c.*1900, and worn in a variety of ways.

Sumptuary edicts laws intended to erect impenetrable fences to preserve the exclusiveness of social status by determining what each rank should be allowed to wear, and to restrict spending for economic reasons.

Surface embroidery decoration of a fabric using a needle and thread, but not producing openwork.

Swiss lace embroidery done by the hand machine, or the Schiffli machine, both of which originated in Switzerland.

Tambour work chain stitch embroidery on a woven fabric, or on net, worked with a tambour hook.

Tatting a knotted lace made with a tatting shuttle, nineteenth century.

Thread a term used in the seventeenth to nineteenth centuries for linen thread, as opposed to silk, metal or cotton.

Tippet *see* Fichu.

Toilet a suite of clothes; a dress and its accessories.

Tønder a continuous bobbin lace made in Denmark and having strong similarities with French Lille and English Bucks point.

Torchon a continuous bobbin lace of geometric design, worked at a 45° angle. Of ancient origin, but revived extensively through Europe in the second half of the nineteenth century.

Tricot a cellular fabric made on the warp-knitting machine, twentieth century.

Tucker a trimming of lace around the neckline of the shift and just showing above the bodice, or attached to the bodice itself, mainly eighteenth century.

Tulle a machine bobbinet, usually of silk; *tulle ruche* – a net gathered and frilled i.e. ruched; *tulle illusion* – a very fine silk net. In French any net or regular background of meshes, whether hand- or machine-made.

Venetian gros point see *Point de Venise.*

Vestee a net or lace panel filling in an open bodice front, sometimes topped with a choker or other collar. Second half of the nineteenth century.

Voile espagnole a Spanish veil, perhaps a kind of mantilla, or a large triangular shawl, 1860s.

Warp Frame originally in the 1780s an attachment to the Stocking Frame enabling it to use many separate threads instead of one single one, and so to produce plain or patterned warp knitting.

Warp knitting knitted fabric in which the loops are made in vertical sequence.

Weft knitting knitted fabric in which the loops are made in horizontal sequence.

Whitework embroidery in white thread on white cloth.

Wholestitch in bobbin laces a stitch in which the threads are very closely compacted so that the work appears like a woven cloth.

Yak a woollen bobbin lace of torchon type made in the East Midlands and elsewhere in the late nineteenth century.

References

(Note: where only the author is given, see Sources and Recommended Reading for details)

Chapter 1, pages 9–24

1 *Oxford English Dictionary:* Fashion.
2 'Ancient Ninevah' in *The Illustrated Exhibitor*, 1852, pp. 145–55, Vol. I.
3 Broholm and Hald, p.30.
4 King, *Before Hansard*, p.4.
5 See Mazzi, in Sources and Recommended Reading.
6 *Argenterie de la Reine*, quoted by Palliser, p.262.
7 1 and 2 Philip and Mary, quoted by Palliser, p.293. They were married in 1554.
8 Great Wardrobe accounts of Elizabeth I, 28–29, quoted by Palliser, p.304.
9 Porteus. *Coins in History*, p.166.
10 Stubbes, quoted by Head, p.109.
11 Quoted by Palliser, p.311.
12 Quoted by Law, *Fleur de Lys*, p.165.
13 André Blum, *Early Bourbon*, Plate 7.
14 Quoted by Head, *The Lace and Embroidery Collector*, 1922, p.114.
15 Fraser, *Mary Queen of Scots*, p.188.
16 John Donne, Nonesuch Library, 1942, p.344.
17 Latour p.2670.
18 Rabelais, *Gargantua*, English translation, Dent, 1933 ed., p.128.
19 Blum, p.5.
20 'Every Man out of His Humour' quoted by Palliser, p.316.
21 Palliser, p.303.

7 Aubrey, *Venetia Digby*, p.189.
8 W. Peacham, *Truth of the Times*, 1638, quoted by Palliser, p.329.
9 Blum, p.13.
10 Cunnington, C. W. and P., *Handbook of English Costume in the 17th century*', Faber, 1966, p.11.
11 King, *Before Hansard*, p.24.
12 Accounts of the Earl of Sandwich, Master of the Great Wardrobe for the Coronation of King Charles II, 23 April 1661, quoted by Palliser, p.335.
13 Thomas Fuller, *The History of the Worthies of England*, quoted by Palliser, p.402.
14 Quoted by Law, *Fleur de Lys*, p.202.
15 See Whiting, pp.64–5.
16 King, *Before Hansard*, p.33.
17 Scott, *Everyone a Witness*, p.160.
18 King, *Before Hansard*, pp.31 and 36.
19 Accounts for haberdashery, lace etc., English manuscripts, 1655–67.
20 Evelyn, *Diary*, pp.110, 144; and *Tyrannus or the Mode*, 1661, quoted by Scott, p.78.
21 Great Wardrobe Accounts of James II, 1685–6, quoted by Palliser, p.340.
22 Boucher, p.281.
23 Pepys, 15 April, 1662.
24 Sévigné, *Lettres*, 21 July, and 11 September, 1680.
25 Palliser, p.44.
26 Quoted by Palliser, p.111.

Chapter 2, pages 25–54

1 Fraser, *Mary Queen of Scots*, pp.59–60.
2 Domestic State Papers of James I, quoted by Palliser, p.319.
3 Blum, p.8.
4 *Oxford English Dictionary:* Lace, 6.
5 'The Trousseau of the Princess Elizabeth (1596–1662)' in *Needle and Bobbin Club Bulletin*, Vol. XI, no. 2, pp.18–28.
6 Domestic Papers of James I, quoted by Palliser, p.378.

Chapter 3, pages 55–75

1 Morris and Hague, *Antique Laces of the American Collectors*, New York, 1926, p.9.
2 Defoe, *The Complete English Tradesman*, 1726, quoted by Palliser, p.171.
3 Cunnington, C.W. and P., *Handbook of English Costume in the 18th century*, Faber, 1972, p.28.
4 Busch, see Sources and Recommended Reading.
5 Emil Hannover, *Tonderske Kniplinger*, Copenhagen, 1974, p.105.
6 Rousseau, *Confessions*, p.252.

7 Walpole, *Correspondence*, 11 November, 1754. Note: 'consideration for the lacemen': the wearing of lace was forbidden during the period of official mourning (about 40 days).
8 Davydoff, *La Dentelle Russe*, Plate I, fig. 11. Note: wild pear trees, *Pyrus cordata* and other species, are often thorny. They are found quite commonly in Europe, though rare in Britain.
9 Walpole, *Correspondence*, 9 September, 1761.
10 Paulis, *Le Passé de la Dentelle Belge*, Appendix, pp.119–25.
11 Hartnell, Norman, *Royal Courts of Fashion*, Cassell, 1971, p.100.
12 Palliser, p.127.
13 Ruth Hayden, *Mrs Delany*, p.63.

Chapter 4, pages 76–100

1 Felkin, W., *History of Machine-wrought Hosiery and Lace*, David and Charles reprint, 1967, p.406.
2 Thompson, Dorothy, *The British People*, p.88.
3 King, *Before Hansard*, p.112.
4 Henson, *History of the Framework Knitters*, p.437.
5 *The Girlhood of Queen Victoria*, 1832–40, Vol. II, Murray, 1912, p.318.
6 Woodham-Smith, p.163.
7 *Everyman's Encyclopaedia*: Exhibitions.
8 Saunders, p.198.
9 From an undated and unacknowledged article entitled 'Lace and Lace-making', *c*.late 1850s, p.26.
10 Saunders, p.75.
11 Law, p.175.
12 Saunders, p.182.
13 Saunders, p.190.
14 *The Englishwoman's Domestic Magazine*, April 1873, p.223.

15 Penderel Moody, A., *Devon Pillow Lace*, Beer, 1907, p.82.
16 Becker, p.476.
17 From a newspaper cutting in the collection of Luton Museum.

Chapter 5, pages 101–115

1 Latour, p.1125.
2 Carita.
3 p.473.
4 Gore Allen, p.183.

Chapter 6, pages 116–133

1 Cunnington, P., and Buck, A., p.104.
2 Cunnington, P. and Lucas, C. *Costume for Births, Marriages and Deaths*, Black, 1972, p.53.
3 John Bulwer, *The Artificial Changeling*, 1650, quoted by Scott, p.78.

Chapter 7, pages 134–144

1 *Oxford English Dictionary:* Drawers.
2 *The Englishwoman's Domestic Magazine*, April 1873, p.224.
3 Hayden, p.125.
4 Cunnington, C. W. and P., *Handbook of English Costume in the 19th century*, Faber, 1959, p.15.
5 *Oxford English Dictionary:* Lingerie.
6 Wright, p.254.

Chapter 8, pages 145–154

1 King, p.5.
2 Godet, Alfred, personal communication.

Sources and Recommended Reading

Abegg, Margaret, *Apropos Patterns for Embroidery, Lace and Woven Textiles*, Berne, 1978.

Addison, J., *Spectator*, 4 vols, Everyman ed., 1907.

Arnold, Janet, 'A Mantua, *c.*1708–9' in *Costume*, No. 4, 1970.

Aubrey's Brief Lives, Ed. Oliver Lawson Dick, Penguin, 1982.

Becker, Bernard, 'Lace-making at Nottingham' in *The English Illustrated Magazine*, May 1884.

Blum, André, *Early Bourbon, 1590–1643*, Harrap, 1951.

Boucher, F., *A History of Costume in the West*, Thames and Hudson, 1967.

Broholm, H.C., and **Hald**, M., *Costume of the Bronze Age in Denmark*, Arnold Busek, Copenhagen, 1940.

Buck, Anne, *Dress in Eighteenth-century England*, Batsford, 1979.

Busch, Ebba, *Mon stertegning til kniplinger, Et ovelseshaefte fra 1700-taller*, Nationalmuseet, Copenhagen, 1980.

Busson, Yvon, 'Les Coiffes de Jadis en Pays Poitevon' in *Modes et Travaux*, No. 972, Nov. 1981.

Caplin, Jessie, *The Lace Book*, Macmillan, New York, 1932.

Carita, *Lacis*, Sampson Low, 1909.

Channer, C.C., and **Roberts**, M.E., *Lace-making in the Midlands*, Methuen, 1900.

Coulton, G.G., 'The Meaning of Medieval Moneys' in *Social Life in Early England*, pp.208–23, Routledge and Kegan Paul, 1961.

Cronin, Vincent, *Catherine*, Collins, 1978.

Cronin, Vincent, *Louis and Antoinette*, Collins, 1974.

Cunnington, Phillis and **Buck**, Anne, *Children's Costume in England, 14th to 19th century*, A and C Black, 1965.

Danieli, Bartolomeo, *Vari designi di Merletti*, Bologna, *c.*1639.

Davis, Adèle, 'The Discovery of a Rare Eighteenth-Century Fan' in *The Fan Circle International Bulletin*, No. 30, 1985.

Davydoff, Mme Sophie, *La Dentelle Russe*, Leipzig, 1895.

Dayot, Armand, *Louis XIV*, Paris, 1909.

Dentelles et Broderies dans le Mode Française du XVI à XX siècle, Musée du Costume, Paris, 1964–5.

Dreger, Moriz, *Entwicklungs-Geschichte der Spitze*, Vienna, 1910.

Earnshaw, Pat, *A Dictionary of Lace*, Shire, 1982.

Earnshaw, Pat, 'English Lace: Cottage, Commerce and Court' in *The Period Home*, June 1981.

Earnshaw, Pat, 'The Wearing of Lace' in *The Period Home*, October, 1982.

Evelyn, John, *Diary*, Ed. de Beer, 6 vols, Clarendon Press, 1955.

Filbee, Marjorie, *A Woman's Place*, Ebury Press, 1980.

Fraser, Antonia, *Mary Queen of Scots*, Weidenfeld and Nicolson, 1969.

Gudjónsson, Else, *The National Costume of Women in Iceland*, Reykjavik, 1978 reprint.

Hayden, Ruth, *Mrs Delany*, British Museum, 1980.

Hemert, Maria von, *The Needlework of the Island of Marken*, Arnhem, 1978.

Hénon, Henri, *L'industrie de tulles et Dentelles mécaniques dans le pas de Calais, 1815–1900*, Paris, 1900.

Henson, Gravenor, *History of the Framework Knitters*, David and Charles reprint, 1970, (1st pub. 1831).

The Illustrated Exhibitor, Vols I and II, Cassell, 1852.

King, Horace, *Before Hansard*, Dent, 1968.

Hudson Moore, N., *The Lace Book*, Chapman and Hall, 1905.

Latour, A., 'Lace Fashion through the Ages' in *CIBA review*, 73, p.2670, Basle, April 1949.

Laver, James, *Early Tudor, 1485–1558*, Harrap, 1951.

Law, Joy, *Fleur de Lys*, Hamish Hamilton, 1976.

Levey, Santina, *Lace: a History*, Maney, 1983.

Locke, John, *Some Thoughts Concerning Education*, 14th ed., Whiston, London, 1772.

Luynes, Duc de, *Mémoires sur la Cour de Louis XV*, Ed. Dussieux Soulie, Paris, 1861.

Mazzi, C., 'La Casa di Maestro Bartolo di Tura' in *Bullettino senesa di Stovia Patria*, Siena, 1900.

Mitford, Nancy, *Mme de Pompadour*. Hamish Hamilton, 1954.

Morris, F., 'Laces of the American Colonists in the 17th century' in *Needle and Bobbin Club Bulletin*, 1926.

Morris, F., and **Hague,** M., *Antique Laces of the American Collectors*, New York, 1926.

Palliser, Mrs Bury, *History of Lace*, Sampson Low, 1910 edition.

Parasole, Isabetta Catanea, *Fiore d'ogni Virtu*, Rome, 1610.

Passarotti, Aurelio, *Libro de Lavorieri*, Bologna, 1591.

Paulis, L., *Le Passé de la Dentelle Belge*, Brussels. n.d.

Pepys, Samuel, *Diary*, Ed. R. Latham, 11 vols, Bell, 1970–83.

Porter, Roy, *English Society in the 18th century*, Lane, 1982.

Porteus, John, *Coins in History*, Weidenfeld and Nicolson, 1969.

Queen Lace Book, Pt. 1, 1874.

Risselin-Steenebrugen, M., *Trois Siècles de Dentelles*, Brussels, 1981.

R.M., *Nuw Modelbuch, Allerley gettungen Dantelschnur ... zubereit*, Christoph Froschauer, Zurich, 1561.

Rousseau, Jean-Jacques, *Confessions*, Wm. Glaisher, London, n.d.

Rousseau, Jean-Jacques, *Emile ou de l'Education*, Paris, 1964 ed.

Ruppert, J., *Le Costume, II et III*, Flammarion, 1931.

Saint-Simon, Louis de Rouvroy, duc de, *Mémoires complets et authentiques du duc de Saint-Simon sur le siècle de Louis XIV et la Régence*, Paris 1840–4 ed, 20 vols.

Saunders, Edith, *The Age of Worth*, Longmans, 1954.

Schuette, Marie, 'Techniques and Origin of Lace' in *CIBA review*, 73, p.2675.

Scott, A.F., *Everyone a Witness: the Stuart Age*, White Lion Publications, 1974.

Sessa, Giovanni-Battista and Marchio, *Le Pompe*, Venice, 1557.

Sévigné, Marie de Rabutin-Chantal, Marquise de, *Lettres*, Paris, 1953–7 ed. 3 vols.

Snelling, Thomas, *A View of the Coins at this time Current throughout Europe*, London, 1766.

Squire, Geoffrey, *The Observer Book of Costume*, Warne, 1975.

Stubbes, Philip, *The Anatomie of Abuses*, 1583.

'Tønder Lace' in *Needle and Bobbin Club Bulletin*, Vol. VII, No. 2, 1923; and Vol. X, No. 2, 1926.

Treadwin, Mrs C., *Antique Point and Honiton Lace*, Ward, Lock and Tyler, 1874.

Vavassore, Giovanni Andrea, *Esemplario di Lavori*, Venice, 1532.

Viccars, R., *A Succinct History of Buckingham Lace*, Peter Robinson, 1884.

Vinciolo, Frederico, *Renaissance Patterns for Lace, Embroidery and Needlepoint*, Dover reprint, 1971, 1st pub. 1587.

Walpole, Horace, *Correspondence*, 39 vols, Oxford University Press, 1939.

White, Cynthia, *Women's Magazines 1693–1968*, Michael Joseph, 1970.

Whiting, Gertrude, ed., 'La Revolte des Passemens, Paris, 1660–1'. Reprinted with translation into English in 1935 from *Needle and Bobbin Club Bulletin*, vol. 14, 1930.

Woodham-Smith, Cecil, *The Great Hunger, Ireland 1845–9*, Hamish Hamilton, 1962.

Wright, Thomas, *The Romance of the Lace Pillow*, Olney, Bucks, 1919.

Index